HOW TO PASS PROFESSIONAL LEVEL PSYCHOMETRIC TESTS

HOW TO PASS PROFESSIONAL LEVEL PSYCHOMETRIC TESTS

Sam Al-Jajjoka

KOGAN PAGE

First Indian Edition 2003

Kogan Page India Private Limited
2/13 Ansari Road
New Delhi 110 002.

ISBN 81-7554-194-6

Rs. 150.00

Published by Vinod Vasishtha for Kogan Page India Private Limited, 2/13 Ansari Road, Daryaganj, New Delhi 110 002, and Printed at Raj Press, R-3 Inderpuri, New Delhi – 110 012.

I dedicate this book to my parents for their everlasting love

Contents

Preface

Before we begin, I would like to give you some of my personal tips on passing and preparing for your assessment day or interview.

Before you attend an assessment day, either visit your favourite library or career service or browse the Internet and do some research on the employer and industry that you are considering. Always keep in mind that employers want to see what you can offer; this is why they have invited you for interview in the first place. The current job market may be the most competitive in recent history; there are simply too many applicants for the well-paid, skilled positions available and it is difficult for an employer to choose from the thousands of candidates. It pays to be well prepared.

Make sure you proofread all your writing carefully before mailing. Have your CV and covering letter read by others. If you find yourself rushing to get something in the post, take a moment to slow down and make sure you are sending out high-quality information, because remember that the employer has to sift through thousands of such applications, and yours must stand out. A scruffy application creates a bad impression. Your career is in your hands.

The employer needs to feel that you took the time and effort to target their company specifically, that you take a special interest in working for them and that you have the abilities and personal qualities to do the job. This is why employers nowadays place such a strong emphasis on psychometric tests as a part of their selection procedures; they use them as a way to measure an applicant's skills. Psychometric tests identify your strengths and weaknesses in relation to the vacancy on offer. They measure whether you have specific abilities or appropriate personal qualities in relation to the job specification, and whether you need further training to develop the necessary attributes. Such testing is usually much more effective than interview alone, according to most psychologists. The accepted view is that putting all the candidates through the same test is a fair way to make a final judgement, but alternatively lots of intelligent people may be excluded if their success is to depend on a 20–30-minute test. However, we are living in the real world and Human Resources departments want to produce statistics so that when you call for feedback on your interview they can tell you how you scored compared with other candidates. In this way you are satisfied as you have proof of whether or not you performed to meet the organization's requirements. The employer is also happy because they can argue from a fair position in awarding the job.

If you are unfamiliar with psychometric tests you may be too nervous to do justice to yourself and may waste valuable time just trying to understand what you are being asked to do. You will certainly be at a disadvantage compared with candidates who have already had practice with such tests. This is where this book comes in. It provides you with intelligent tips and helpful hints that could help to get you a job offer.

I hope this book enhances your understanding of psychometric tests, and that familiarizing yourself with the different tests will give you the courage and self-confidence to improve your performance.

Acknowledgements

It was a hard job to find spare time and energy to write this book. However, I would like to thank my software engineer colleagues in Germany and my students in the UK who motivated me to write it, since psychometric tests are becoming so popular and there are insufficient books to help candidates to practise and familiarize themselves with such tests before their assessment day.

Introduction

This book contains examples of the type of aggressive psychometric tests which may be encountered in IT, management and finance recruitment procedures, although some tests (Chapters 1, 2 and 4) are of relevance to other areas of employment too. The book is designed to work in tandem with other publications from Kogan Page, now used by thousands of students. The book assumes that you have been invited for interview or to an assessment centre, and are now preparing yourself for the big day.

However, even if you have never been invited for interview or to an assessment centre before, you will do just fine. This book is designed to be used as a guide to testing your abilities and brain power, to assess your strengths and weaknesses. It also makes the daring assumption that you are somebody special; there are too many books written for every possible candidate, so this book is tailored for strong performers like you.

The selection process varies for individual jobs and the number of psychometric tests available in the market is enormous. The ones included in this book are based on my personal experience from talking to my students and attending interviews and assessment centres for large and small organizations. Psychometric tests are gaining a global significance; in my previous job in Germany I discovered that such tests are becoming part of selection procedures there. The book provides step-by-step assistance and intelligent tips to help you perform better, and if you follow my methods of approaching problems, as presented in this book, you can greatly increase your chances of being selected. The book in your hands is about passing certain tests on your assessment day. I have taken the utmost care to provide relevant exercises, currently in common use. The book is designed to give you confidence in taking any kind of psychometric test through preparation and familiarization with what is required. Although I cannot guarantee that all your tests will be exactly like the ones given here, I have tried to provide examples of the main kinds, so you can expect to meet something quite similar.

The book focuses on the most popular tests used to select people best suited for professional positions, depending on the skills needed in the job. Other tests such as verbal aptitude tests, quantitative reasoning tests, personality questionnaires (to see how you would react or behave in different situations), written exercises to demonstrate your written communication skills, and interviews which allow you to demonstrate oral communication skills are often included in the selection procedures of large organizations. For this reason, I suggest you read other Kogan Page publications to prepare fully for interview or assessment.

It is always a good idea, before an interview, to call the human resources department or ideally the person who contacted you and ask what sort of tests you will be required to undertake. Some organizations even send a simple flyer with some practice examples included in your invitation letter. This is only to give a flavour of what you should expect; it does not mean that only similar tests will be used. While it is sensible to concentrate on those tests, I have known of instances where an organization gave advance warning of only two tests, but surprised candidates on the day with another one never mentioned in their invitation letter or telephone call. Therefore, I recommend that you spend some time reading all the chapters and understanding all the exercises and tips presented here, so you will be less likely to get a shock on your assessment day.

The investment of time and effort to study the book and familiarize yourself with the types of questions that may be asked and tips for approaching them is an investment in your future. Take the time to read through most, if not all of the exercises in this book; there may be some that apply to your assessment day.

Furthermore, while the exercises in this book are useful in teaching you the basic skills, feel free later on to deviate from them and build your own examples. Let your examples evolve. They will in all probability get better and better as your brain starts adjusting to a new challenge. It is like learning a new language. It is difficult to say a word or express your ideas at the beginning, but then you become fluent and able to produce your own speech. Confidence and speed come with determination to do better, and with practice and familiarization.

What are psychometric tests?

Psychometric tests are multiple-choice questions (this does not necessarily apply to all the tests in this book) to be answered within a set time (and the timing is very tight) using usually pencil and paper, but they can be on a computer. They are designed to assess a wide range of your abilities and whether you have specific skills in relation to the job specification or position for which you are being considered. The questions, in principle, need no further study or prior knowledge and are based on your logical reasoning or thinking performance. Of course, the more skills are being tested, the more psychometric tests you will be required to perform and the more accurate and comprehensive will be the picture of you built up by the employer. A typical test has a time limit allowing you between 25 and 60 minutes for 30 to 120 questions. Each question typically has only one correct answer, which is often to be selected from 3–5 alternatives (although tests exist that require more than one suggested answer to be identified as correct). Therefore, every incorrect alternative successfully identified and eliminated improves your chances of choosing the correct answer from the alternatives remaining. The questions are designed to become more difficult as you go through and are designed not to be completed within the given time unless you are a genius!

My advice is to read the instructions in each test, make sure you understand the practice examples provided at the beginning of the test, ask the assessor to clarify any ambiguity, and then work through the questions as quickly and accurately as possible. Start with the ones you can answer accurately and, if you are taking too long over a question, move on to the next one; if you have time you can go back later to finish the ones you did not manage to answer. Remember you don't get extra marks for finishing early, and it is only the number of correct answers that counts. Sometimes negative marking is used, which means that you lose marks for incorrect answers. If this is the case, don't use guesswork to fill in your score sheet and try your best to answer correctly as many items as possible. However, if negative marking is not used, I advise the use of intelligent guessing to improve your score, by eliminating all the incorrect choices and making random guesses on the remaining ones.

Usually your results are compared with those of other candidates who have done the test in the past, which is called the norm group. In this way, the company will able to assess your skills in relation to others, and to make a judgement about your ability to cope with tasks involved in the job. If you take many psychometric tests during one assessment day, it is usually your overall performance that is important. However, this is not always the case, as I found out with one organization; when they sent the overall score sheet to one of my students his overall score was a pass, but in two of the tests he scored less than the minimum required, and was in consequence not invited for the next stage.

Even if you don't feel confident about your performance in the psychometric tests, there are other forms of assessment and you may have other strengths (eg group exercise or writing skills), which will be taken into account and might compensate for your weakness. Finally, always, even if you fail, ask the employer for feedback about your performance. This may help you to pinpoint your weaknesses in order to work on them in the future and learn from the experience; it may also aid you in deciding your career path.

General remarks about your psychometric test day

- Discuss your test with your career adviser (if you have one), who might suggest you sit a timed practice test prior to your actual test day. Such practice is nowadays available in most universities to give you some feedback on your performance, so you know what you should work on before the actual test.
- Acquainting and familiarizing yourself with what is required, by hard work and practice prior to the test, will help you to improve your performance.
- Avoid being nervous; believe in yourself.
- At the beginning of each test, you are given a couple of examples to ensure you know what you are required to do. Don't hesitate to ask the assessor to clarify the instructions and remove any ambiguity.
- The best way to choose alternatives in multiple choices is to eliminate all wrong answers and use your judgement to choose the best answer from the remaining ones.
- Work as quickly and accurately as you can and avoid taking too long over a question; however, if you still have time left, go back to sort it out.

Psychometric Tests often Encountered in IT or Finance Recruitment

Diagrammatic reasoning using the alphabet

In this test you are shown a number of diagrams representing an input→transformation→output process in which the input is altered by rules depending on commands, which are represented by symbols. Your task is to identify the rule represented by each symbol, based on the information in the diagram, and to apply these rules to the input data you are given. Different rules may be used for the same symbol in different diagrams. Therefore, consider each diagram on its own and work out what rule each symbol stands for: don't generalize the rules for the whole test. No two different symbols have the same rules in the same diagram. As a rule of thumb, always follow the arrow for input and output for every path independently. Table 1.1 shows some of the common rules used in alphabetic diagrammatic reasoning. It is intended only to give an idea of what to expect. However, other possibilities are left to your imagination.

Table 1.1 Some common alphabetic diagrammatic reasoning rules

Input	Output	Comment	
1	ABCD	ABC	delete right
2	ABCD	BCD	delete left
3	ABCD	ABD	delete third from left
4	ABCD	ACD	delete second from left
5	ABCD	DABC	last is first
6	ABCD	BCDA	first is last
7	ABCD	ABDC	exchange the position of the last two characters
8	ABCD	ACBD	exchange the position of the middle two characters
9	ABCD	DCBA	move sequence to the front
10	ABCD	DBCA	exchange the first and last
11	ABCD	ABCDF	add a new character F to the sequence
12	ABCD	AABCD	add similar character to the first
13	ABCD	ABCE	change the last character to the next letter in the alphabet
14	ABCD	CDAB	exchange every two characters from left to right

TIPS

Consider the example shown in Figure 1.1 and follow the rules as one way to solve the problem.

- Identify the shortest path by following only one input and output path. In Figure 1.1 we have three paths; paths 1 and 2 are the shortest and path 3 is the longest.
- Identify all the identical symbols; if identical symbols appear in one figure, they must obey the same rules.
- Work out the shortest path rules, ie path 1 and path 2 using Table 1.1 as your guide, as shown in Figure 1.2. As you can see, once you have figured out the rules for one symbol you can apply the same rules straightaway to other similar symbols in the same diagram. By doing this you will save time.
- In any one figure, two different symbols do not have the same rules.
- Finally, go back to the longest path 3 and, as you can see, you are left to find out the rules for only one symbol, #. Again, consider the common rules introduced in Table 1.1 in conjunction with the other symbols as shown in Figure 1.2.

Figure 1.1 Illustrates the three paths

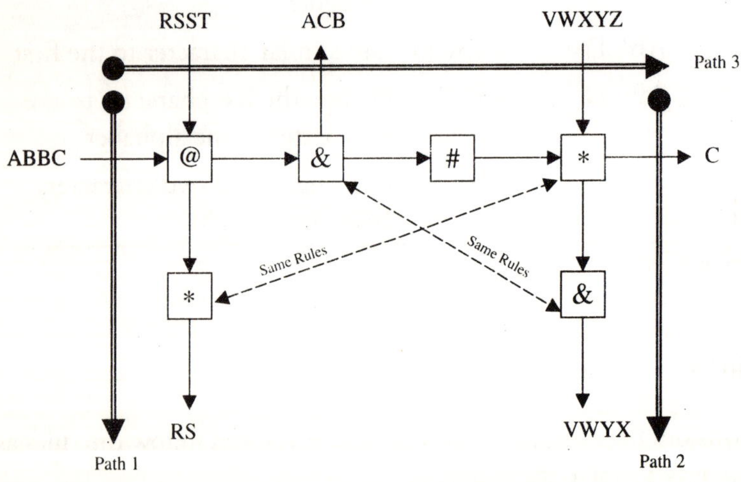

Figure 1.2 Shows step-by-step solution

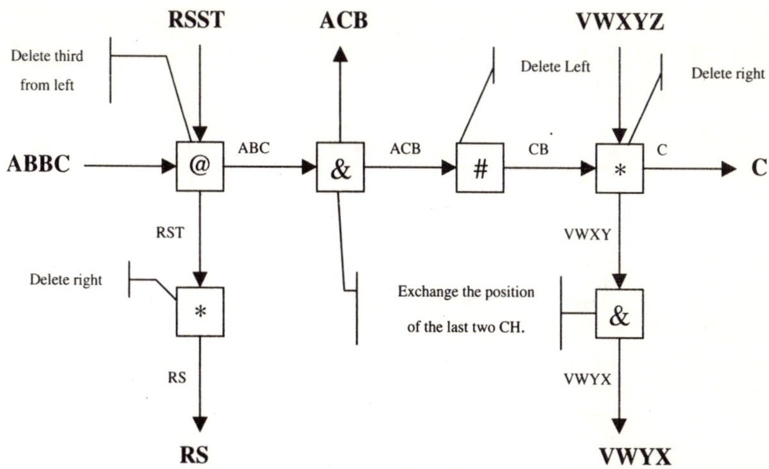

Once you have mastered the basics, try to define your own symbols and rules and devise new figures to suit your ability and convenience. However, I am sure that as you become more familiar with the diagrams you will be able to create your own way and devise a new method to solve the problem, which suits your ability.

Now try the following practice questions, as shown in Figures 1.3 to 1.9, which contain 40 questions. Marking your answers on scrap paper, see how many questions you can do in 30 minutes.

Diagrammatic reasoning using shapes

In this case you are shown a number of diagrams in which a shape (in a square box) is altered by a command represented by a symbol (we use similar symbols as before; however, they are put in circles rather than squares). Table 1.2 shows some of the common rules used, just to give you an idea of what you should expect. Be aware that these are not the only possibilities.

Figure 1.3

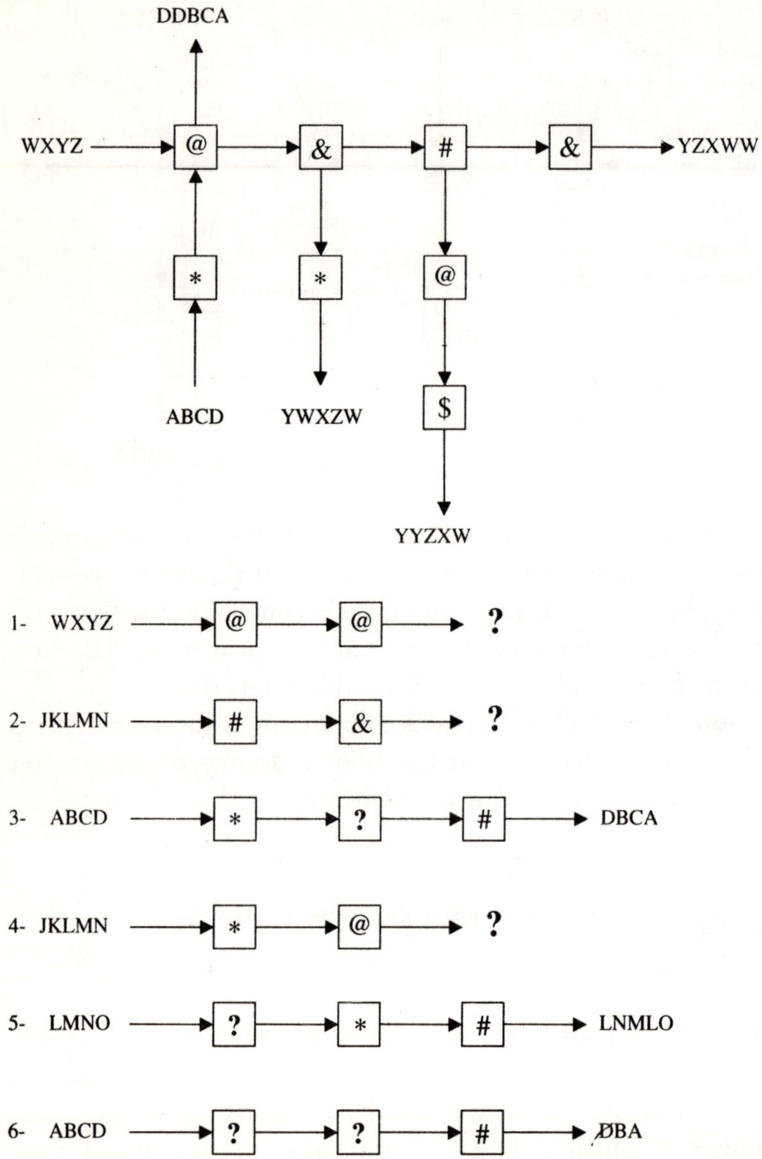
DDBCA
WXYZ
@
&
#
&
YZXWW
*
*
@
ABCD
YWXZW
$
YYZXW
1- WXYZ
@
@
?
2- JKLMN
#
&
?
3- ABCD
*
?
#
DBCA
4- JKLMN
*
@
?
5- LMNO
?
*
#
LNMLO
6- ABCD
?
?
#
DBA

Figure 1.4

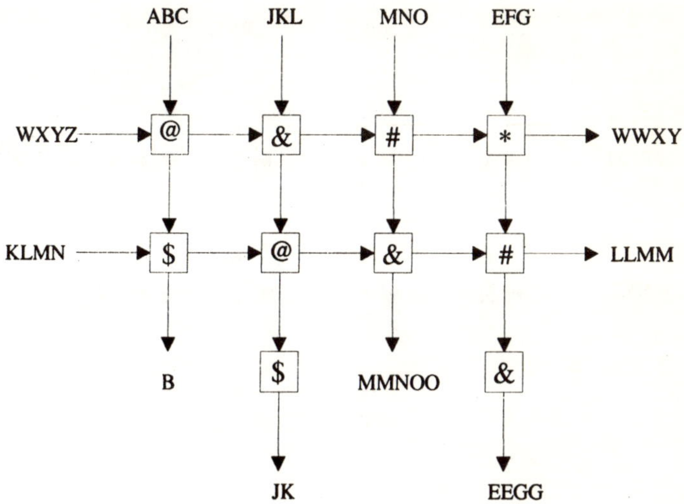

7- ABC → @ → # → ?

8- MOP → ? → & → # → MMOO

9- EFGH → ? → ? → * → EEEFH

10- ABC → & → * → ?

11- OOPP → @ → ? → # → OPP

12- JKLMN → * → @ → ?

Figure 1.5

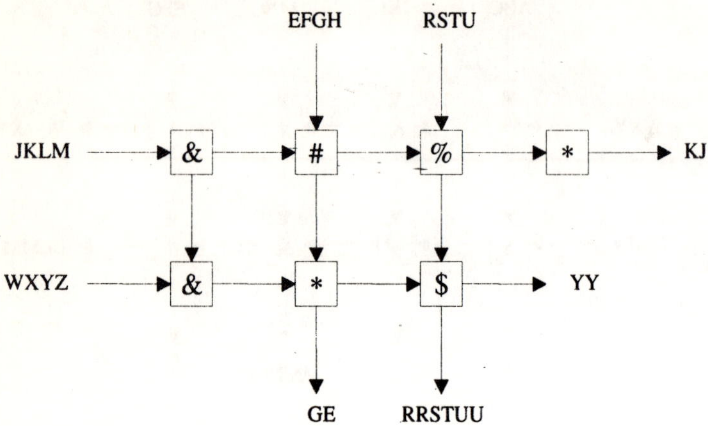

13- ABCD → & → ? → ABCC

14- ABCD → # → % → ? → BCA

15- ABCD → * → # → & → ?

16- ABCD → % → ? → * → BCDD

17- ? → $ → # → ACBAD

18- BBA → $ → # → ? → BBAA

Figure 1.6

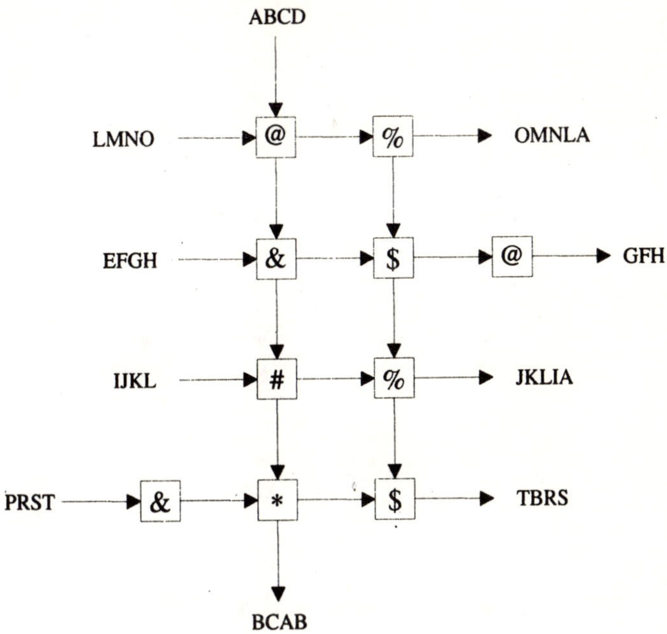

19- LMNO → % → * → ?

20- VWXY → # → $ → % → ?

21- ABCD → & → * → @ → ?

22- ? → $ → # → QRS

23- ANA → $ → # → # → ?

Figure 1.7

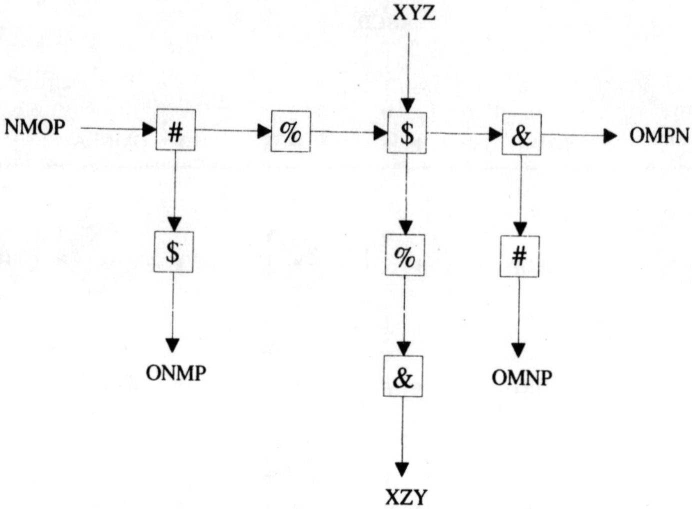

24- ABC → $ → # → ?

25- MNOO → ? → & → # → NOOM

26- XYZZ → # → & → % → ?

27- POQR → $ → ? → # → PORQ

28- OOPP → % → ? → # → OPPO

29- JKLM → & → $ → ?

Figure 1.8

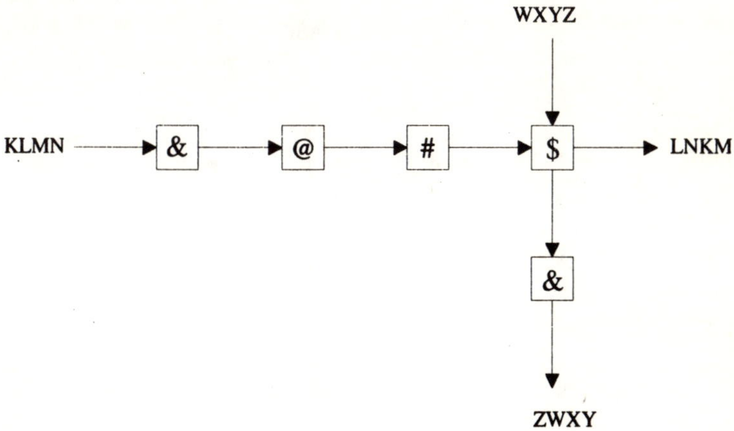

30-

31-
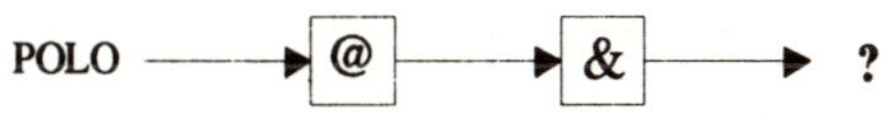

32-

33-
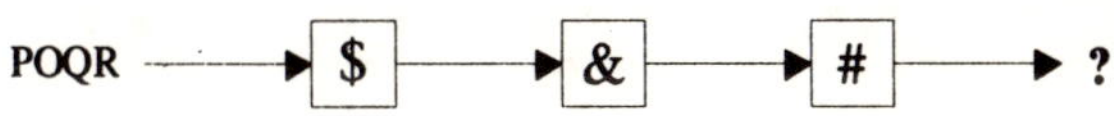

34-
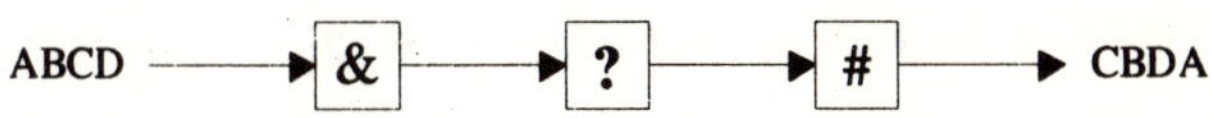

35-
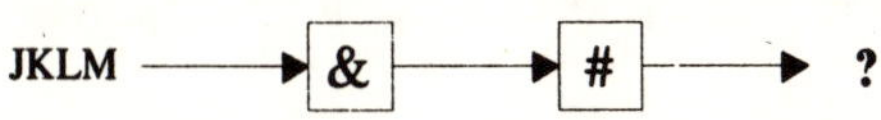

Figure 1.9

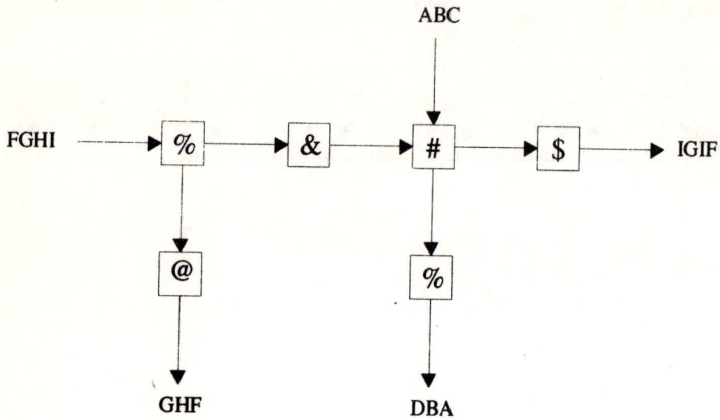

36- FGHI → $ → # → ?

37- QRST → ? → & → % → SRT

38- VWXY → # → & → @ → ?

39- OOTR → $ → & → ? → ROTO

40- OOPP → % → ? → # → OPP

Table 1.2 Some of the common rules used in diagrammatic reasoning using shapes

	Shape	Altered	Comment
1		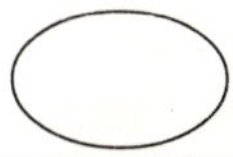	Change of size
2			Change of colour
3			Change of shape
4			Rotate to any angle
5		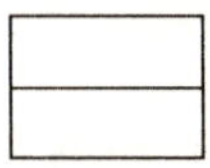	Add Horizontal line
6		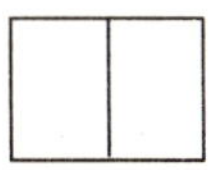	Add Vertical line
7			Turn only the colour upside down

TIPS

Consider the example shown in Figure 1.10 and follow the simple rules below as one way to solve the problem.

- Identify the shortest path by following only one input→ output path. In Figure 1.10 we have only two equal paths to consider at the same time. Follow the rules represented by each symbol and see the solution in Figure 1.11.
- Identify similar symbols; since they are in one diagram, they must obey the same rules. However, a symbol may well have a different meaning in another diagram; therefore avoid generalization in your test.
- In any one figure, two different symbols do not have the same rules.
- The same symbol may appear twice in a sequence in a single diagram. The symbol may, for example, convert the shape from square to circle, but the second time the same symbol converts it back again, which is different from the rules used in diagrammatic reasoning using the alphabet.

Figure 1.10 Shows the two paths

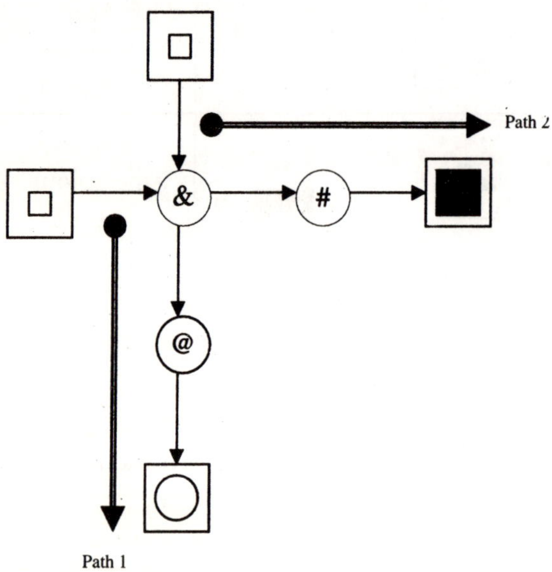

Figure 1.11 Shows the solution of the above example

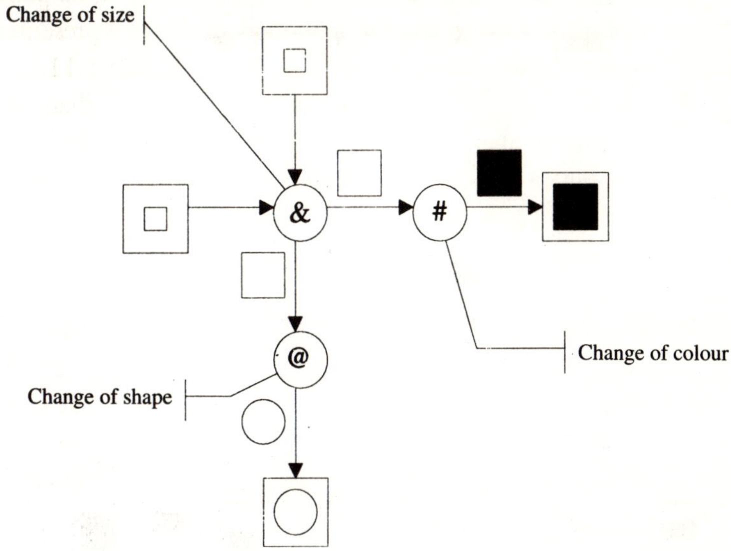

However, I am sure that as you become more familiar with the diagrams you will be able to create your own way and devise a new method to solve the problem, which suits your ability.

Now try the following practice questions as shown in Figures 1.12 to 1.15, which contain 24 questions. Mark your answers on scrap paper and see how many questions you can do in 15 minutes.

Figure 1.12

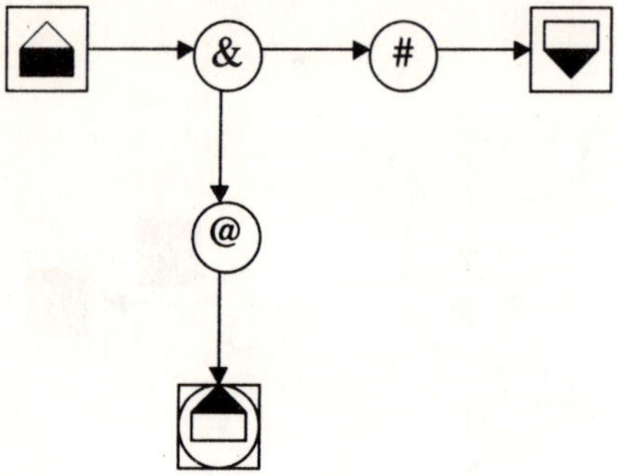

A B C D

41- 

42- 

43- 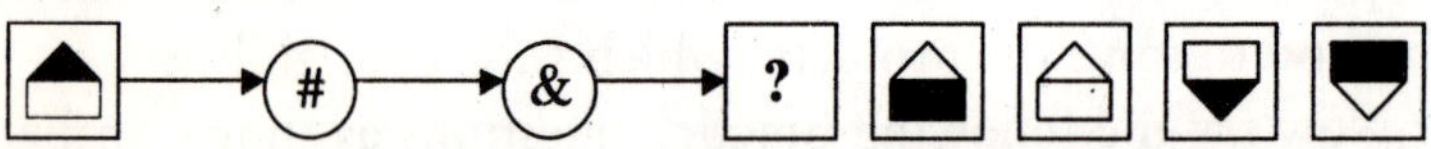

44- 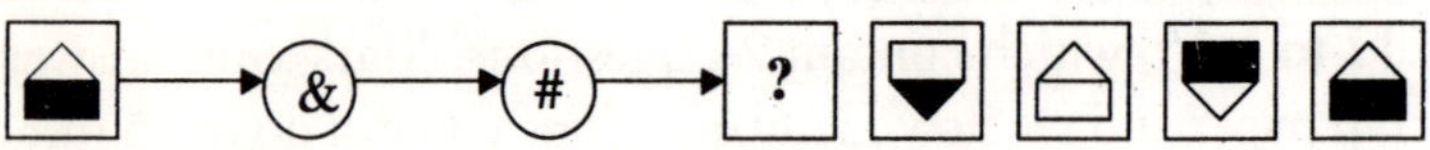

45- 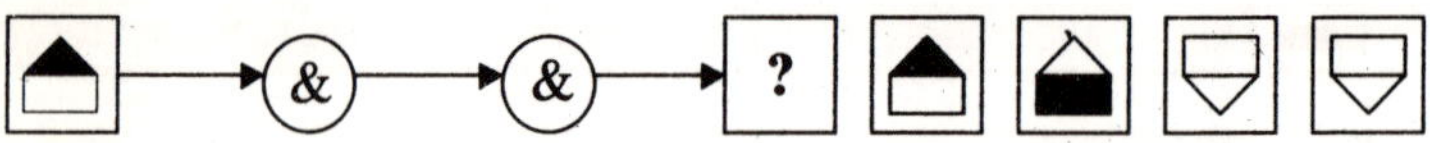

46- 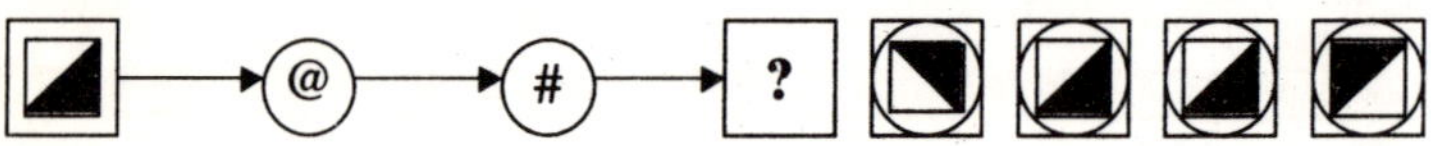

Figure 1.13

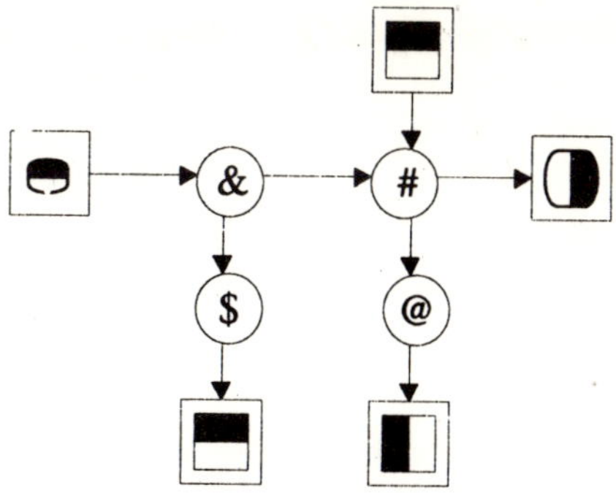

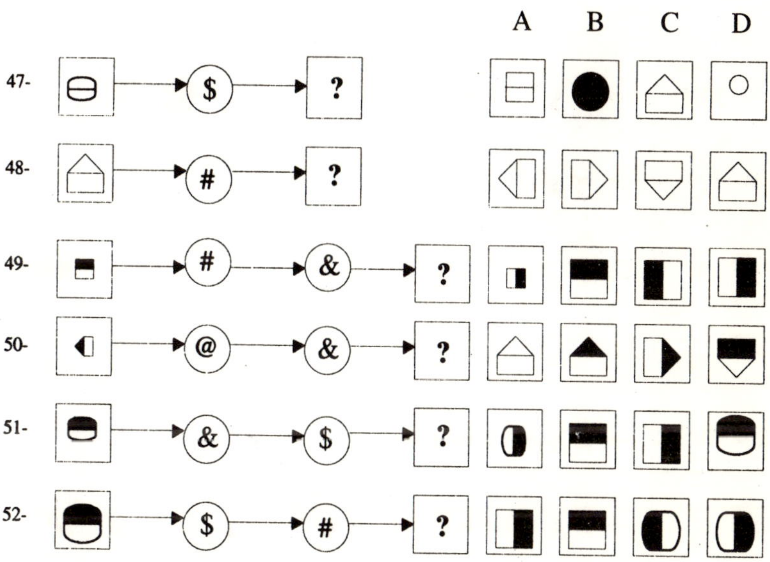

Figure 1.14

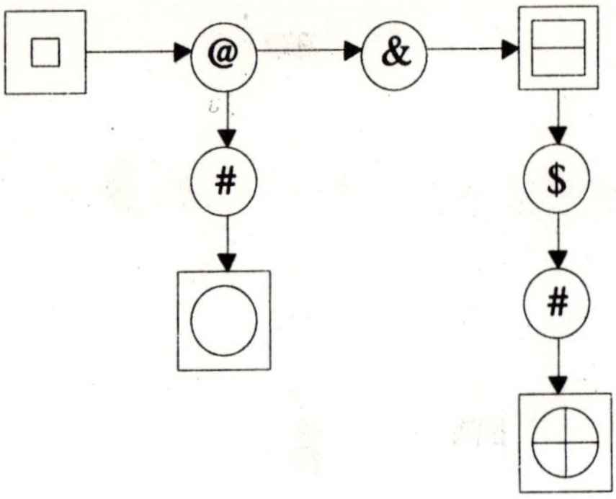

A B C D

53- 

54- 

55- 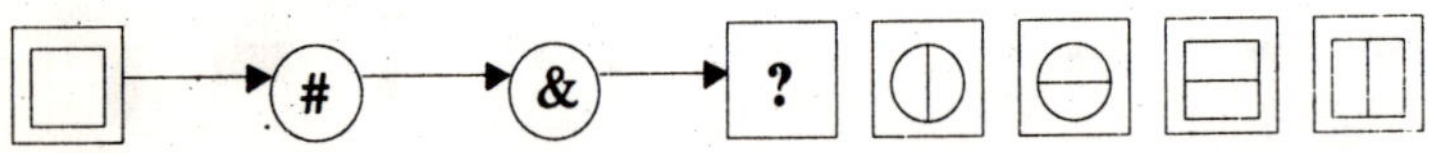

56- 

57- 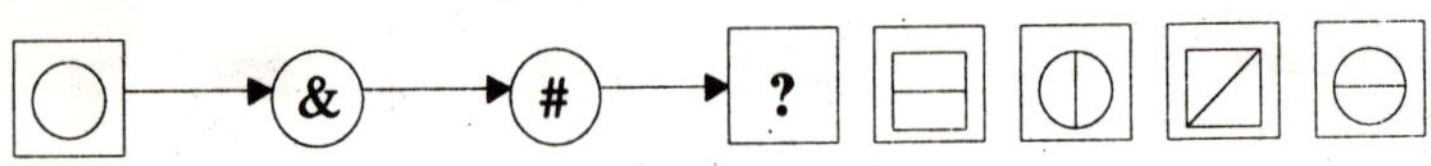

58- 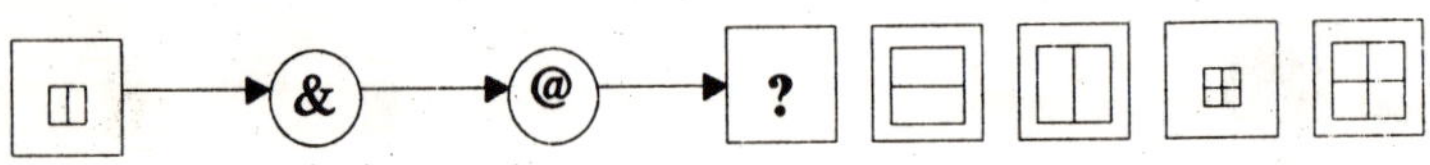

Figure 1.15

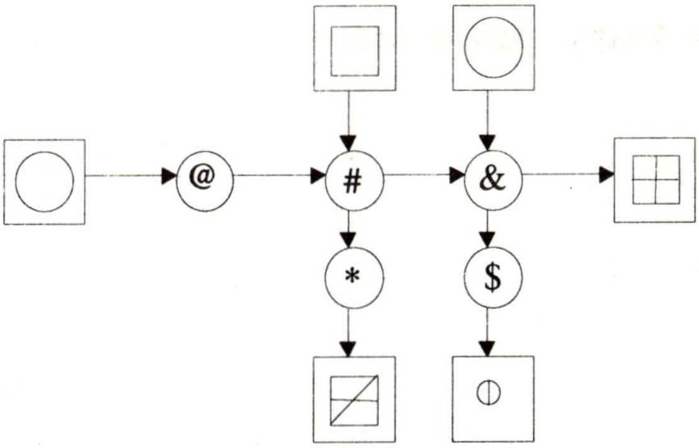

A B C D

59- 60- 61- 62- 63- 64-

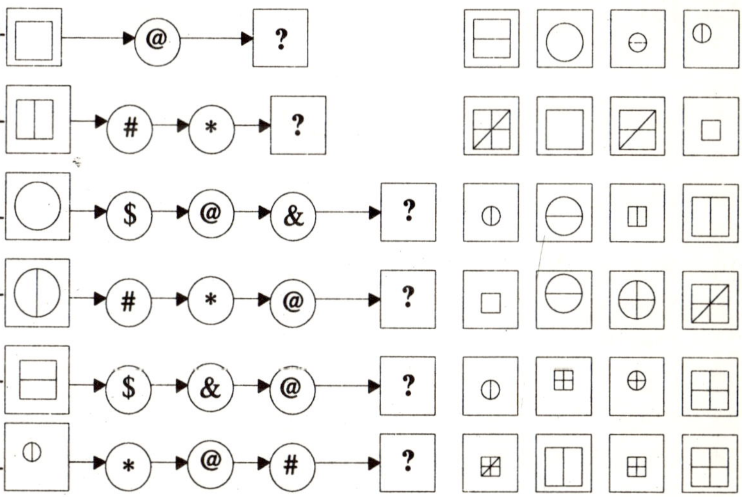

Answers to Chapter 1

Practice tests (page 10)

1. WWWXYZ
2. NMLJK
3. #
4. NNKLMJ
5. @
6. &, $
7. ABB
8. @
9. &, &
10. AAC
11. $
12. JKL
13. $
14. *
15. D
16. $
17. DCBA
18. #
19. BLMNOA
20. VWXYA
21. DBCB
22. QRS
23. NAA
24. CBA
25. %
26. XZZY
27. &
28. $
29. JKLM
30. LMN
31. LPOO
32. $
33. QRPO
34. @
35. KLMJ
36. GHIG
37. @
38. VWX
39. %
40. @
41. A
42. C
43. D
44. A
45. A
46. A
47. A
48. B
49. D
50. D
51. B
52. A
53. D
54. A
55. B
56. C
57. A
58. D
59. B
60. A

61. C
62. D
63. C
64. A

Solutions for all diagrammatic reasoning tests (page 10)

Figure 1.3 solution

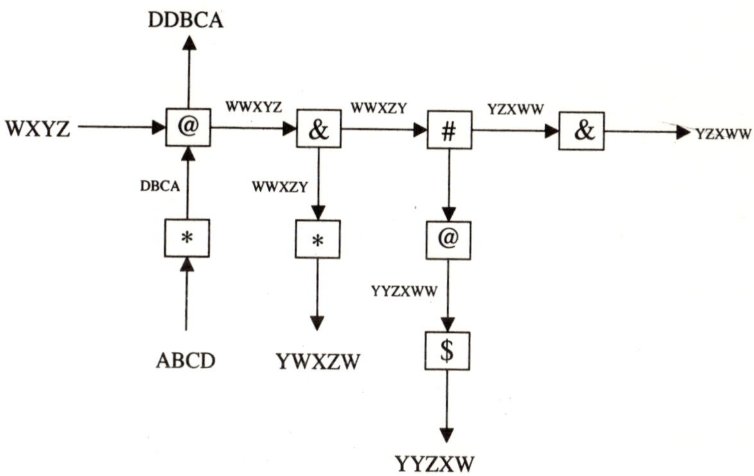

Figure 1.4 solution

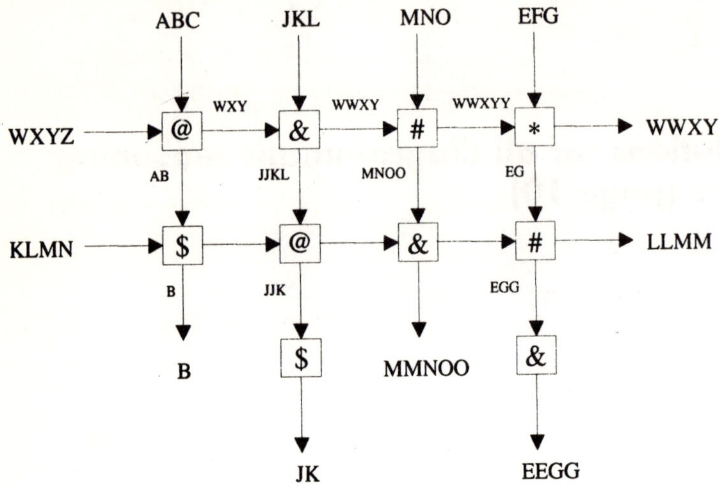

Figure 1.5 solution

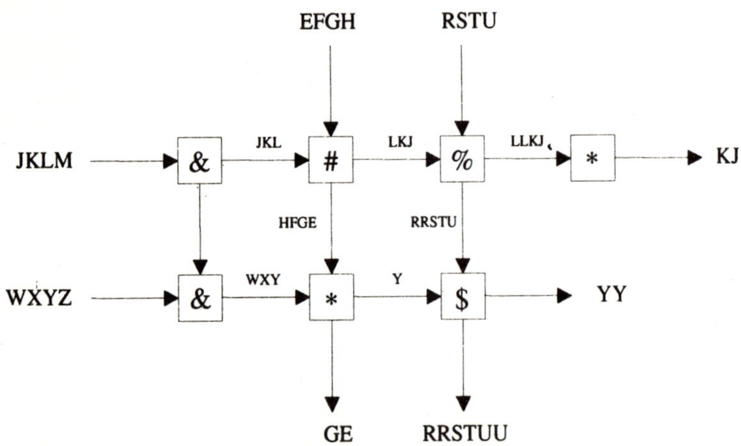

Figure 1.6 solution

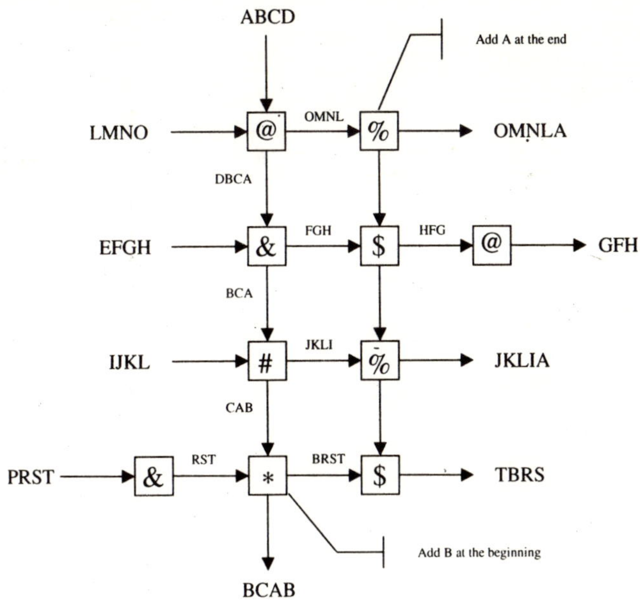

Figure 1.7 solution

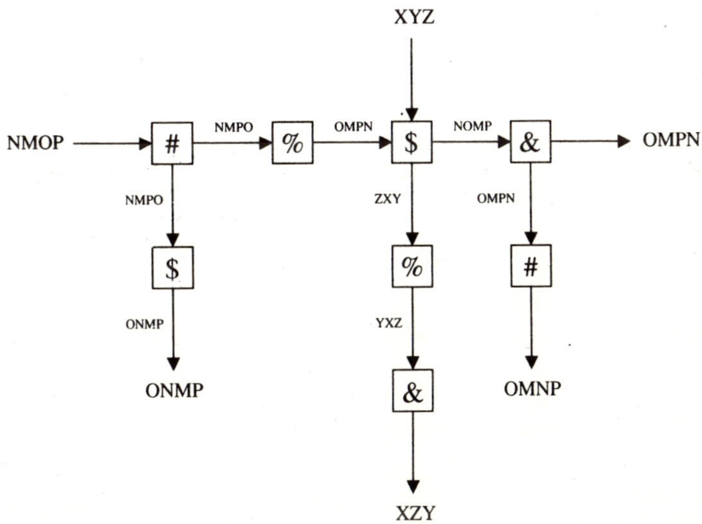

Figure 1.8 solution

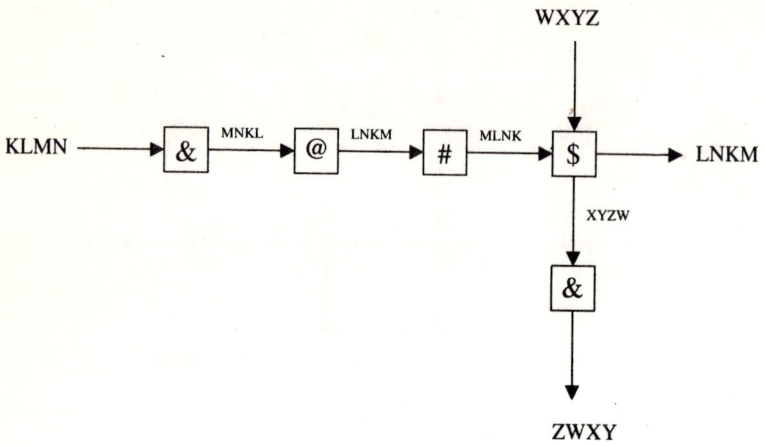

Figure 1.9 solution

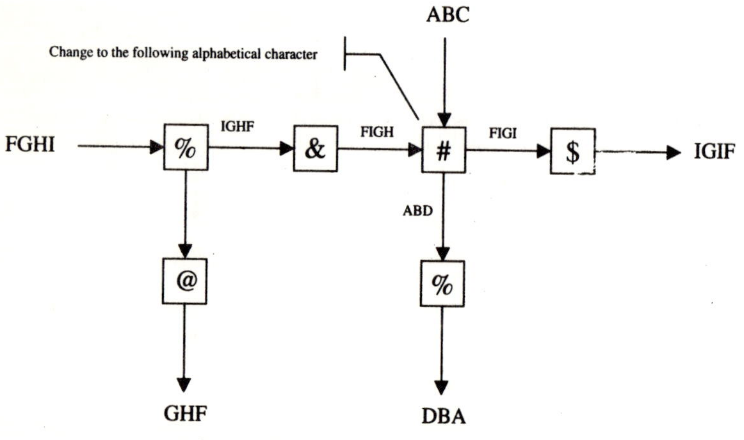

Figure 1.12 solution

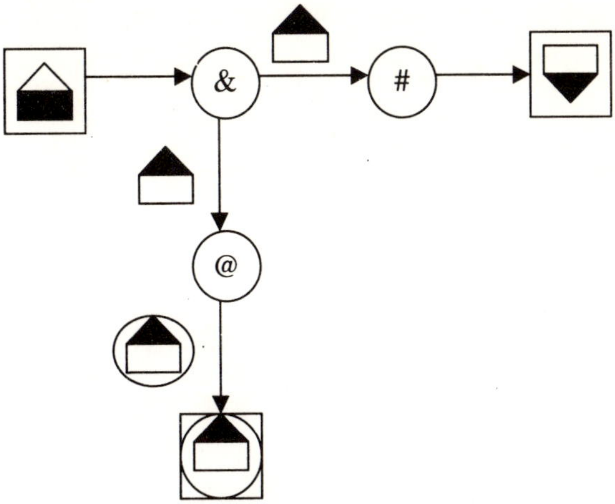

Figure 1.13 solution

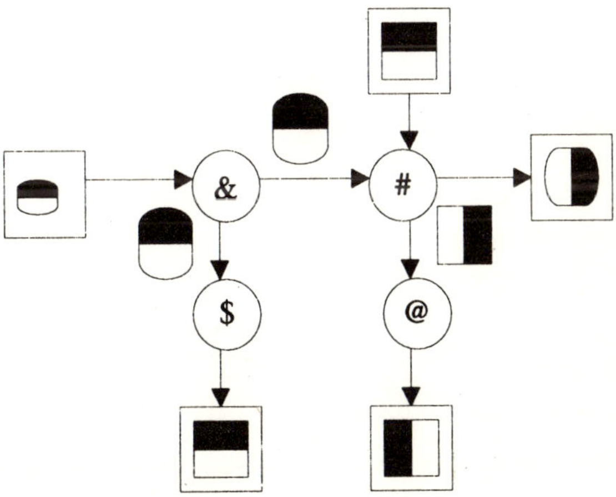

Figure 1.14 solution

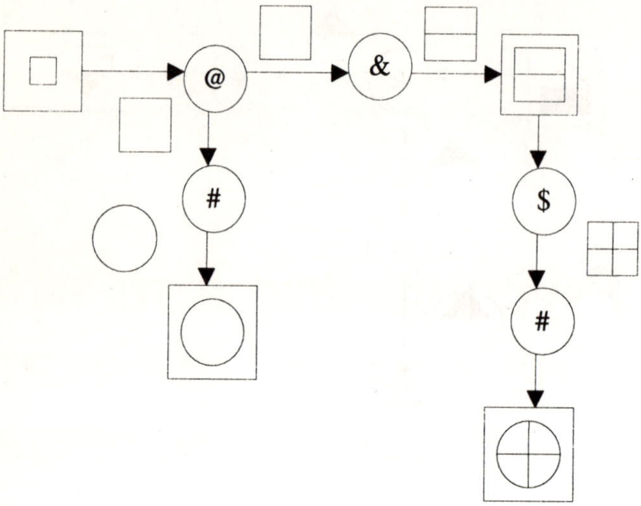

Figure 1.15 solution

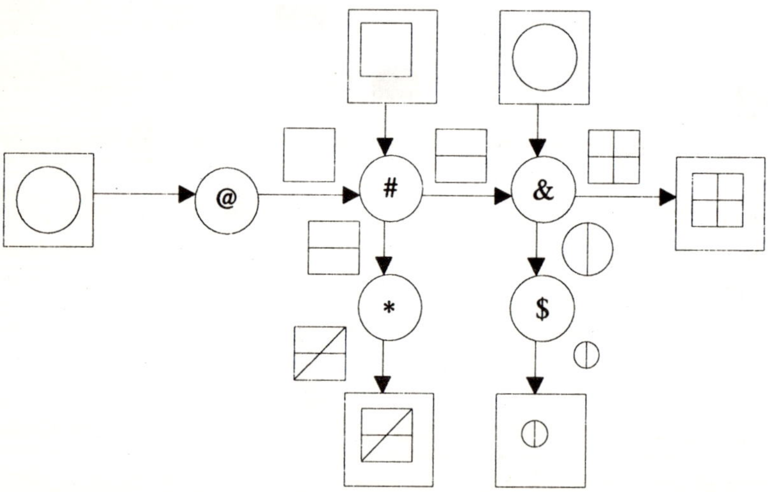

2

Psychometric Tests often Encountered in Finance and Management Recruitment

Character series

Character series is one of the tests commonly used by big organizations instead of number series. Therefore my advice is to be prepared for both, in case the organization does not tell you which one they will use. Books from the Kogan Page series, such as *How to Pass Numeracy Tests* and *How to Pass The Civil Service Qualifying Tests*, are definitely a good source for number series tests. In this test you will be presented with a character series and asked to find the correct rules and complete the series. A series can start from any point in the alphabet (A–Z) and you have to work out which sequences to use.

TIPS

For many candidates, character series tests offer the opportunity to add extra points to their overall performance during the assessment day. Write the alphabetical series (A–Z) on a separate scrap of paper to help you visualize the order of all the characters and then work out the sequences as quickly and accurately as possible. I personally wrote the sequences about five times during the practice session on separate pieces of paper, so if I marked one erroneously, I would already have another one available without using a rubber. Look at the examples below.

Example 1

	1	2	3	4	5
X Y X Y X Y X Y	**X**	**Y**	**Z**	**V**	**W**

For this example, the series goes: XY XY XY
The next letter in the series is X, choice 1.

Example 2

	1	2	3	4	5
V V W W X X Y Y	**U**	**S**	**T**	**Z**	**Q**

In example 2 above, the series goes like this: VV WW XX YY
The next letter in the series is Z, choice 4.

Now try example 3 below and indicate the correct answer on a separate piece of paper.

Example 3

	1	2	3	4	5
V J W J X J Y J	L	M	Z	O	P

In example 3, the series goes: VJ WJ XJ YJ

Therefore, the correct answer is Z, choice 3. Finally, do example 4 and indicate the correct answer, which is one of the letters at the right side of the page.

Example 4

	1	2	3	4	5
a b c d a b c d a b c	d	a	b	c	e

In example 4, the series goes like this: abcd abcd abc

Therefore, the correct answer is d, choice 1.

When you are ready and confident that you have understood the concept above, try the 36 questions and allow yourself 8 minutes to finish.

Practice questions

															1	2	3	4	5
1	B	B	C	D	D	E	F	F							C	H	G	K	I
2	M	S	M	T	N	S	N	T	O						O	T	S	P	M
3	J	K	L	J	K	L	M	N	O						M	N	O	P	Q
4	K	L	M	K	L	N	K	L	O						M	N	O	K	P
5	A	B	L	M	N	A	B	O	P						R	S	M	N	Q
6	A	B	C	V	A	B	C	W	A	B	C	X			A	B	C	Y	Z
7	M	N	O	P	Q	O	R	S	O	T	U	O			T	V	W	X	Y
8	q	p	o	q	p	o	q	p	o	q	p	o			o	p	r	s	q
9	U	V	V	W	X	X	Y	Z							Z	V	W	X	Y
10	h	t	u	q	r	s	h	t	u						s	u	t	q	h
11	a	b	d	e	g	h	j	k							l	m	n	o	p
12	K	L	M	M	N	O	P	P							Q	R	S	T	U
13	A	V	W	B	X	Y	C								A	X	Y	Z	V
14	p	p	r	r	t	t	v	v							x	y	z	v	a
15	I	I	I	H	H	G	F	F	F	E					G	H	E	F	D
16	C	D	C	D	A	B	E	F	E	F	A	B			K	G	H	I	J
17	I	J	J	K	K	K	L	L	L						O	K	N	L	M
18	R	Q	P	O											M	O	P	L	N

															1	2	3	4	5
19	J	K	L	S	T	M	N	O	S	T					Q	P	R	S	T
20	o	q	s	u											v	t	o	w	x
21	r	s	t	r	s	t	u	r	s	t	u	v			t	s	r	x	w
22	r	s	r	t	u	t	v	w	v	x	y				y	x	z	w	t
23	W	W	X	W	X	Y	Y	Z	Y						Y	X	Z	W	V
24	N	X	O	P	X	Q	R	S	X						S	T	U	V	Q
25	a	c	f	j											p	o	n	m	r
26	K	L	N	O	R	S									W	X	V	U	T
27	m	p	n	q	o	r	p								t	u	v	r	s
28	o	u	p	v	q										v	p	w	x	y
29	E	H	L	O	S										W	X	Y	V	Z
30	C	D	E	F	G	I	J	K	L	N	O	P			R	S	T	U	V
31	D	G	I	L	N										P	Q	R	S	T
32	k	p	u	l	q										u	v	w	t	x
33	u	a	r	d	o										f	h	g	k	l
34	A	L	M	B	P	Q	C								R	S	U	T	V
35	A	B	X	C	D	Y	E	F							Y	W	H	G	Z
36	Q	W	P	X	O	Y	N								Z	X	R	S	T

Logical pattern and sequences

This is the ability to think strictly logically in abstract terms. In this test you are given a row of four figures on the left-hand side of the page and four figures on the right-hand side of the page. The four figures on the left-hand side contain several symbols, patterned in a logical sequence, and you are asked to discover how the sequence is constructed and how it works. When you have found that, you have to complete the logical sequence with one and only one figure from the right-hand side of the page on the same row. Look at the example below.

Example 1

The answer is B, as there have to be five lines in the square (first square one line, second square two lines, third square three lines, and so on).

Example 2

The answer is B, as the triangle movement is 90 degrees anti-clockwise. The next or fifth position would thus be pointing upward.

Example 3

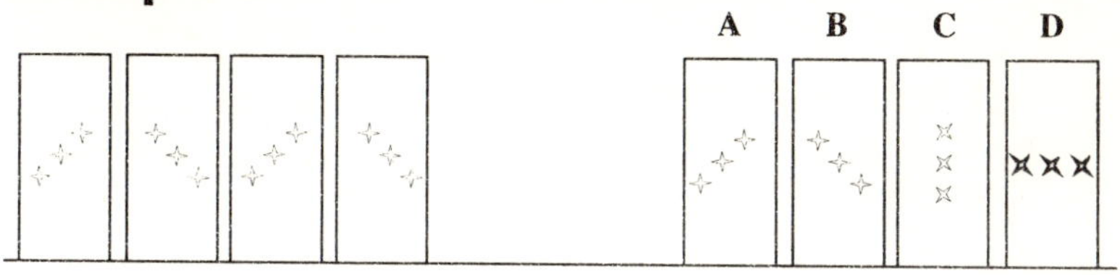

The answer is A. The stars form alternate diagonals.

When you are ready and confident that you have understood the concept above, try the 25 questions below and allow yourself 5 minutes to finish.

Table checking

Usually, very little time is allowed in tests of this kind: between 8 and 15 seconds per question, depending on the test and the company providing the test. Therefore, it is important to work quickly and accurately. Depending on which company is providing the test, there are many ways in which the test can be presented. What is given here is a flavour of what you may get in your actual test, and I leave it to your creativity to design further examples and set the time limit to meet your ability. However, I will mention here, briefly, a few examples from the popular formats. The test could be presented in the form of an original column with items, eg a string of characters, symbols, etc, to compare with a typed copy that differs from the original organized in single columns; you have to pinpoint the differences.

A B C D

1 

2 

3 

4 

5 

6 

7 

8 

9 

10 

11 

12 

13 

A B C D

14

15

16

17

18

19

20

21

22

23

24

25

Example 1 Single column

Original	Typed copy
A B C D 5 E 6 F 7 G 8 H 9	A B C D 5 6 F 7 G 8 H 9

As you can see from the above example, the character E is missing in the typed copy.

In another form you would have to compare the first column string of letters and numbers with a number of copies in different columns and again mark the mistakes in each column, as shown below.

Example 2 Multiple columns

Original	Copy 1	Copy 2	Copy 3	Copy 4
X Y Z % T &	Z % T &	X Y Z &	X Y Z % T &	X Y % T &

As you can see, XY is missing in the first column (copy 1), % and T are missing from the second column (copy 2), there are no mistakes in copy 3 and Z is missing from copy 4.

Another type involves comparing sets of characters or symbols arranged in pairs, one on the left and another on the right, and pinpointing how many pairs are identical in a single question.

Example 3 Arranged in two pairs

ILOVE	ILOV
SD&M7	SD&M7
ROTOR	ROTOR

In the above example, two of the three given pairs are identical.

Another way is to identify the identical pair from several columns on each row.

Example 4 Identify identical pair from among many columns

A	B	C	D	E
XYZ232	XYZ332	XYZ234	XYZ232	XZY232

For the above example we have only one identical pair in columns A and D. Of course, in all of these examples you will be provided with a separate sheet on which to mark your answers.

TIPS

Valid for only Example 4 models; I took the test below myself and saw the benefits. My advice is to take four or five letters or numbers (depending on your ability) from the beginning or end of column A and compare with the rest. When you find the matches, compare the remaining character(s). The choice of four letters is optional and could be from any column. See the diagram below.

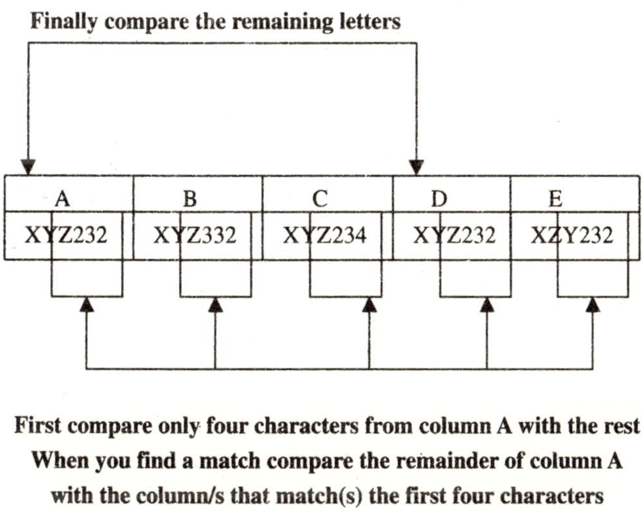

When you are ready and confident that you have understood the concept above, try the test below and allow yourself 7 minutes to finish. Mark the two identical sets of letters or numbers of the appropriate columns (A, B, C, D, E or F) on a separate answer sheet.

	A	B	C	D	E	F
1.	XNM23%	XNL23%	MXN23%	NXM23%	XNM32%	XNM23%
2.	1*$2RTY	12*$RTY	1*2$RTY	1*2$RYT	1*2$RTY	1*2R$TY
3.	OPQ65K	OPQ56K	OQP56K	OPQ56K	QOP56K	KOPQ56
4.	XCVBN	XCVBN	XCBVN	XCVNB	XVCBN	XCBNV
5.	LNM$*W	LNM*$W	MN*$WL	LMN*$W	LMN$*W	LMN*$W
6.	GHI49!	HGI4=9!	GHI4=9!	GHI4=!9	GHI4=9!	GHI=49!
7.	TRE&R%	TRER&%	TER&R%	TRE %	TRE&R%	TR&ER%
8.	DCE?R*	CDE?R*	CDE?R*	CDE? *R	CED?R*	CDER*?
9.	TIR6532	IRT6532	ITR5632	ITR6523	ITR6532	ITR6532
10.	JQ&W80$	JQW&80$	JQW&08$	JQW&80$	JQW&8$0	QJW&80$
11.	A*D65&	A*D6&5	A*D65&	A*D56&	A D *65&	A*65 D &
12.	#4T&(R*	#4T&R(*	#4TR& (*	4#&R(*	#4T&R(*	4#T& (*
13.	8Q5TH?	QT85H?	Q85T?H	Q85TH?	Q58TH?	Q85TH?
14.	2 M ^$5K	M2^$ K 5	M2^5$K	M2^$5K	M2^$5K	M^2$5K
15.	0LO4K%	0LKO4%	0LKO4%	0LOK4%	0LK4O%	L0KO4%
16.	VW8$42	WV48$2	VW4$82	VW48$2	VW48$2	WV482$
17.	TRL9#%	TRL9%#	TRL9#%	RTL9#%	TR9#L%	TR9L%#
18.	KL4&#W	KL4#&W	K4L&#W	KL4&#W	KWL4&#	L4K&#W
19.	POI7834	PIO7834	PO7I834	POI7483	POI7384	POI7834
20.	?3ERNV	?83ERVN	?83ENRV	?8E3RNV	?83ERVN	?8ERNV
21.	FLE9@4	LEF9@4	LFE9@4	LF9E@4	LFE94@	LFE9@4
22.	OTR731	OTR71	OT731	OR731	OTR731	ORT71
23.	OP?\24%	PO?\24%	OP\?24%	OP?2\4%	OP?\24	OP?\24%
24.	XC8*L?3	X8*L?3	X8C*L?3	XC8L*?3	XC8*L3?	XC8*L?3
25.	MN$%L9	MN$%L9	MN%L9	ML N%$9	NM$%9	MN$%L9
26.	56P78H$	56P78$H	56P87H$	5P678H$	56P78H$	65P78H$

	A	B	C	D	E	F
27.	%M&7*T	%M7&*T	M7% &*T	%M7*T&	%M7&*T	%M7&T *
28.	#OYT%	#YT*%	#OYT*%	#OYT*%	#OT*%	OYT*%
29.	PTR68!	PR68!	TPR68!	PTR86!	PTR68!	TRP68!
30.	TR6&231	TR6&321	TR63&21	TR6&321	TR&621	TR6&31
31.	E4R5T6G	4ER5T6G	E4R56GT	E4RT56G	E4R5T6G	EG4R5T6
32.	O15REW	OT4REW	0T5RWF	OT5REW	OT5REW	OT5RFW
33.	IT&D*$	IT&D*$	IT&D$*	T1&D*$	IT&D$	ITD*$
34.	LKD579	L5KD97	LK5D97	LDK597	LKD597	LKD597
35.	QSA&$T	QAS&$T	AQS&$T	QAS&T$	QAS$T	QA&$T
36.	9RT67	69RT67	69R67	6RT67	69RT67	6RT76
37.	JDSETI4	JDSTI4	JSETI4	JDSET4	JDSETI	JDSETI4
38.	M56&$	N56$	NM56$&	NM6&$	NM56&$	NM56&$
39.	JTRLNOP	JTLNOP	JTRLNOP	JRLNOP	TRLNOP	JTRLNP
40.	139587&	1-39587&	1-3587&	1-3957&	1-3958&	1-39587&
41.	985HTR4	985TR4	985HTR4	85HTR4	95HTR4	985T4R
42.	TR24&*	TR47&*	T247&*	TR247&*	TR247&*	TR247&
43.	QR%8H	Q%#8H	QR%#8H	QR%#8H	QR#8H	QR%#8

Answers to Chapter 2

Character series (page 34)

1. 2
2. 3
3. 1
4. 4
5. 5
6. 1
7. 2
8. 5
9. 1
10. 4
11. 2
12. 1
13. 4
14. 1
15. 3
16. 2
17. 4
18. 5
19. 1
20. 4
21. 3
22. 2
23. 3
24. 2
25. 2
26. 1
27. 5
28. 3
29. 4
30. 1
31. 2
32. 2
33. 3
34. 4
35. 5
36. 1

Logical pattern and sequences (page 38)

1. B
2. C
3. A
4. D
5. A
6. B
7. C
8. D
9. A
10. C
11. A
12. B
13. C
14. D
15. A
16. C
17. B
18. A
19. B
20. C
21. D
22. C
23. B
24. A
25. B

Table checking (page 42)

1. A and F
2. C and E
3. B and D
4. A and B
5. D and F
6. C and E
7. A and E
8. B and C
9. E and F
10. B and D
11. A and C
12. B and E
13. D and F
14. D and E
15. B and C
16. D and E
17. A and C
18. A and D
19. A and F
20. B and E
21. C and F
22. A and E
23. A and F
24. A and F
25. B and F
26. A and E
27. B and E
28. C and D
29. A and E
30. B and D
31. A and E
32. D and E
33. A and B
34. E and F
35. B and C
36. B and E
37. A and F
38. E and F
39. A and C
40. B and F
41. A and C
42. D and E
43. C and D

3

Psychometric Tests for IT Recruitment

High-level programming language test

Owing to the shortage of well-qualified IT specialists, most companies nowadays recruit people from all walks of life. It is not necessary to have know-how or qualifications in IT subjects, only the desire and the ability to think logically are required. Most industries offer intensive courses in different high-level programming languages, eg Java, C, Pascal, etc, and it is a matter of time before you become an expert programmer.

High-level languages are geared towards the people writing the program rather than the computer. These languages provide the interface between the user and the machine. They are as close to English as you can get and easy to program since their operations closely resemble the language in which the problem is formulated, rather than the internal computer architecture. However, they are sufficiently scrupulous to allow the computer to translate the program written in the high-level language into machine language. The translation of a program written in high-level language into machine language is accomplished by means of a special computer program called a compiler. Since each computer system has its own machine language, a different compiler is required for each high-level language. The compiler checks your program for errors. If there are errors the compiler issues an error message or warning. The compiler checks for a variety of errors, some of which are used here as practice exercises. It is not unusual to have to compile your program many times until all errors have been deleted from it.

In this book I present two kinds of compiler checking. For this exercise you will play the role of compiler to identify the errors in the mock-up programs described below. If you already have some programming skills, be careful not to confuse yourself, because the programs here don't abide by the usual programming rules used in high-level language. Also, be aware that you will have NO time to compile your program more than once, owing to the tight time set for the test. Therefore, you need to pinpoint errors first time and to work quickly and accurately.

Compiler checking by tracking error

In this test you will find a mock-up of unstructured programming lines taken from a C look-alike language, which contain many errors. The errors have been identified and categorized into three types: syntax error (SE), logical error (LE) and other error (OE). Each of the three types of error has its own set of rules. Using these rules, your task is to trace and determine the exact location of an error in each programming line and then identify what type of error it is, ie SE, LE or OE. If no rule has been broken, cross the column No Error (NE).

Look at the following example:

		SE	LE	OE	NE
1.	Printf ("\n Maximum and minimum of the 3 numbers				

Now look at the following set of rules:

SE rules:	LE rules:	OE rules:
A Lines must end in a colon (:).	A Division by zero is not allowed.	A Lines must begin with semi-colon (;).
B Number must be between stars, eg, *7*.	B All arithmetical expressions must be written in upper case eg X=Y+7; X1/Y1.	B Double quotation (") can only be used with Printf statement.
C All characters may be used except @, $.		C Rule A from SE and OE does not apply on the opening brace {.

As you can see, rules A and B in SE have been broken; the line should end in a colon and the number, ie 3, should be between stars. No rules are broken in LE. Rule A has been broken in OE, because of the missing semi-colon at the beginning of the line. Therefore, you should cross the SE and OE columns, as shown below.

		SE	LE	OE	NE
1.	Printf ("\n Maximum and minimum of the 3 numbers	X		X	

Now, try the following exercise. See how many you can complete in 10 minutes, then compare your results with the answers given at the end of this chapter.

	SE	LE	OE	NE
1. ;Include<stdio.h>,				
2. ;Include <math.h>:				
3. #define (NST):				
4. ;double a1b1/x1, Y3				
5. ;main (11Maxim@),				
6. ;{				
7. ;Printf("na="); X/*0*=Y:				
8. ;Scanf(7)%1f, &a):				
9. ,Printf ("%f,*10*);X				
10. ,(* Calculate ymax @ Ymax, "9"):				
11. XM=0.5+X2(Y1–Y2):				
12. ;MAX=OR+T:				
13. ;Printf("\n X=8%, Y=8%8+61),				
14. }				
15. ;Void =X1/Y1+7				
16. {:				
17. ;X1=A+0.5(B–A(NST):				
18. ;Y1=x(R1):				
19. If (y1=y2) Then Y1=8+x				
20. Printf("n Interest Rate");				
21. :For (c=1; c <=20/0;++ c);				
22. ;L=0.01+n,				
23. ,Return:				

	SE	LE	OE	NE
24. ,Scanf("a, @/B):				
25. ;Maximum (x,y):				
26. ;While (N/*0*=X+Y) Then X=Y:				
27. For (count=1; count<=n;count=1+n)				
28. ,Func1(int n):				
29. ;int y=X:				
30. ;X/0=Y:				
31. ;Return:				
32. }				
33. ,Int Funct1 (inta1):				
34. ;(int funct2 (X+Y=2)):				
35. ,B=F($):				
36. ,Return;				
37. ;/initialize and read in a value for /:				
38. ; While x=y calculate the average :				
39. ; AVERAGE=X+T–Y:				
40. ;Read in the number:				
41. ;For "(c=x; c<=n c=n+x)":				

Compiler checking by line rules

In this test you are presented with a mock-up programming language, designed to be similar to Pascal. Here, however, the conditions are set for each individual line, rather than for the whole program, as in the previous example. Your task is to discover which conditions, if any, have been broken. If more than one condition is broken, then you mark more than one column. If no conditions are broken, then mark column Z.

Look at the example below:

		W	X	Y	Z
A	Procedure Admittance (X=7:Real; VAR G, B:Real)				

Now look at the following set of rules:

Conditions for line A in the program:	Conditions for line **B** in the program:	Conditions for line C in the program:
W Lines must end in a *. X Number must be between double quotation, eg, "7". Y All numbers may be used except 5 and 7.	W Lines must begin with the word Return. X All arithmetic expression must be written in upper case, eg X = Y + 2. Y All characters may be used except @ and ?.	W All lines must start with upper case letter. X Double quotation, "cannot be used. Y Number must be between brackets eg (7) + (5).

As you can see, in the example the line is designated by the letter A, so you should look above at the conditions applied to line A. Rules W, X and Y have all been broken: there is no * at the end of the line, the number 7 should be between quotation marks, and number 7 should not have been used. Therefore, you should cross W, X and Y as shown below:

		W	X	Y	Z
A	Procedure Admittance (X=7:Real; VAR G, B:Real)	X	X	X	

Now, try the following exercise. See how many you can complete in 10 minutes and compare your results with the answers given at the end of this chapter.

			W	X	Y	Z
1.	A	Program A1 A2 A3 *				
2.	B	Return (‘Enter Vol Tages A1, A2, @, 5)				
3.	C	If ABS(9) <0 AND ABS>”3”				
4.	B	Return If no signal output then =X+y				
5.	C	For N=0 to end points Do X=Y				
6.	A	Procedure Traprule (B=7) *				
7.	C	Return SUM=SUMY+X				
8.	B	Retur N=Y+K,				
9.	A	Area=SUMOF+H+”4”+J				
10.	B	Writeln (NI=5–X=?)				
11.	C	Trapezoidal =(2)+”8”–(3)= 4;				
12.	B	Return all procedures to zero if possible?				
13.	C	Var V1, V2, V4 are real,				
14.	A	NO=(10–5)=”7”*				
15.	C	Repeat x[M]=NO +(3)				
16.	B	Array X[K] Until X=Y+1				
17.	A	Function data “6” *				
18.	B	Return To the Upper class				

			W	X	Y	Z
19.	C	Procedures solution to all x=@+"1",				
20.	A	Newprogram="9"–"4"+X="5"X				
21.	A	For K=I+1 to I–1 Do				
22.	B	Reteren and then H–K=G+I				
23.	C	Writeln Mean = ' SUM/N' – 8;				
24.	A	Read(data) & SUM=X+Y*				
25.	C	m=N*SUM/N (SUM)				
26.	B	Return U=O+5+7				
27.	A	X,Y: Array[1..3]{1..8},				
28.	C	real array "8"+"3"				
29.	B	Procedure Bestline Return*				
30.	C	Read from (7) To (5)				
31.	A	If Length < "15" then M=N*				
32.	B	If Real AND Imaginary Equal Then X=Y				
33.	C	return(All chartacter+Variables)				
34.	B	While return Y+I=6				
35.	A	Mean=K+T*				
36.	B	Return=X=(9)+K is the total number*				
37.	C	Const A1, 23, "9", ? and(X)				
38.	A	If length >0 and N<8 then *				
39.	B	While X=10 AND Y=20 Then				
40.	A	Write x>"7" FOR ALL y<X *				

TIP

This tip is based on testing a number of my students to see the best way to perform the test quickly and accurately. I found that taking all the programming lines in consecutive order is not a good way, because your brain has to keep switching back and forth between the rules for the three error types, ie SE, LE and OE in compiler checking by tracking error, or the different lines A, B or C in compiler checking by line rules. This wastes time and leads to confusion. The best way is to handle one type of error at a time. Take for example the previous exercise for compiler checking by line rules. Instead of checking line after line, you simply take the conditions set for line A and test every line in the program where line A is identified, and mark your answer if the conditions are broken. When you have done this, look at the conditions for line B, go through the whole program and test all lines marked B, and so on. In this way, there are fewer rules to remember, you are less confused and your brain does not have to switch between conditions, so comparison is more accurate and fast. My students improved by about 70 per cent using this approach. However, practice brings mastery.

Assembly language test

Assembly language is a low-level language that is oriented towards the computer rather than the people who are programming the computer. To use a particular assembly language the programmer must have a thorough understanding of the internal architecture of the central processing unit (CPU) of that particular computer. The language consists of a list of instructions identified by means of mnemonic words and symbols. The number of instructions and commands used depends on the type of CPU, and can be executed only on computers of identical design. Programming is very time consuming to learn and it takes considerable experience to become proficient. Furthermore, programmers are always preoccupied with internal details of the architecture rather than the actual programming task to be accomplished. However, assembly language has a few advantages. First, it runs much faster than high-level language because it is nearer to the fundamental language (machine language, ie writing programs using a series of zeros and ones) for any computer. Second, there are some tasks, which require direct access to hardware architecture, which are more easily implemented by assembly language and probably difficult or impossible to do with high-level language.

Many IT companies are using the basic commands offered by assembly language to develop their own assembly language which is not related to any particular CPU architecture and is only used for testing candidates' computer aptitudes. Most of the commands and symbols used in these tests are very simple if you have previous knowledge of assembly language programming; however, if not, it could be a very challenging experience. IT companies claim in their invitation letters that prior programming knowledge is not required; however, it is difficult to comprehend how a candidate who has a degree in social science, has never programmed before and is interested in making a career in the IT industry can understand the basic programming skills and answer the questions when attending these tests. Usually, no practice exercise is provided or sent to the candidates. During these tests you are given a manual to read and understand how the instructions of the given assembly language operate and a booklet with questions to answer. Usually the answers require you to write a simple program of between 2 and 10 lines. The test is designed to test your logical ability to read and understand material on a new programming language quickly and to work under pressure, to write as many programs as possible correctly.

In this section you will learn a few basic rules regarding look-alike assembly programming. The important and most common elements are presented, which will be useful in assisting inexperienced programmers to minimize mistakes during the actual test.

To familiarize yourself, read all the examples and solutions provided. But don't forget, in your actual test, to follow the command rules given, which may differ from those in the examples given here.

Structure of assembly language

Most assembly languages contain the following basic elements:

- registers identified to store your variables;
- various mnemonics representing the basics of arithmetic (addition, subtraction, etc);
- various mnemonics to perform other programming operations such as subroutines or loops.

A brief description of the most common commands is given in Table 3.1. However, bear in mind that these commands don't belong to any particular CPU and are used here to let you understand what you might expect in your real test.

TIPS

As mentioned before, these tests tend to be very easy if you have some programming skills. However, the examples below and the provided test-solutions are a very good starting point to familiarize yourself with what to expect. I cannot recommend any particular book because most are written for a specific CPU architecture; nevertheless, it may help you to look at one (it doesn't matter which) to see the extensive list of commands.

In most of these tests you are required to perform simple mathematical operations, including counting and looping, and follow the simple rules:

Table 3.1 Basic common commands

Mnemonic	Function	Result
MOV	MOV A, 2	Load register A with 2, ie A = 2
	MOV I,10	Or allocate I = 10,
ADD	ADD A, 2	Add 2 to register A content, ie A = A + 2
	ADD A, B	Add A to B, ie A = A + B
SUB	SUB A, 2	Subtract 2 from register A content, ie A = A – 2
	SUB 2	Subtract previous operation by 2
MUL	MUL A, 2	Multiply register A by 2, ie A = A * 2
DIV	DIV A, 2	Divide register A by 2, ie A = A / 2
CMP	CMP A, B	Compare the contents of A and B, ie A = B, A < B or A > B.
	CMP 2	Compare previous operation with 2.
JMP	JMP endfile	Jump to the endfile position. Endfile could be the label for start another program called Subroutines.
JMPZ	JMPZ endfile	Jump to the endfile position if the previous calculation is zero
JMPE	JMPE endfile	Jump to the endfile position if the previous calculation is equal
INC	INC A	Increment register A by one, ie A = A + 1
DEC	DEC A	Decrement register A by one, ie A = A – 1

Note: In all the above commands, only one variable can be operated on at one time. So 3M, for example, consists of two variables 3 and M, which should be operated on, or implemented, separately.

- Simplify algebraic expressions by performing the operations inside parentheses first and reduce a fraction to the lowest possible terms before writing your program, ie the numerator and denominator have no common factors. For example, 8/12 + 8/6 = 24/12 = 2. This final result should be used in your program.
- Multiplication/division must be programmed first, then addition or subtraction.
- Usually, a single storage register is allowed to store a single operand at one time. Therefore, before performing any mathematical operation using the second operand, make sure which operand you should express first as shown in the example below:

ADD A, B	A = A + B
ADD B, A	B = B + A

- Use the JMP command in most comparison expressions.

A brief description of these basic command elements is provided in the example below.

Example 1 Arithmetical instructions

	MOV A, 6	A = 6
	ADD A, 4	A = 6 + 4 = 10
	INC A	A = A + 1 = 10 + 1 = 11
	DEC A	A = A – 1 = 11 – 1 = 10
	SUB A, 6	A = A – 6 = 10 – 6 = 4
	MOV B, 8	B = 8
	ADD A, B	A = A + B = 4 + 8 = 12
	SUB A, B	A = A – B = 12 – 8 = 4
JMP	Finish	The program will jump to the label called Finish and leave the rest of the program

```
End:    MOV  Result, 0      Result = 0
        ADD  Result, A      Result = Result + A = 0 + 12 = 12
        SUB  B, Result      B = B – Result = 8 – 12 = – 4
Finish: ADD  A, B           A = A + B = 4 + 8 = 12
JMP     End                 The program will jump back to
                            the label called End.
```

Example 2

Write a program using the basic commands described in Table 3.1 to evaluate the arithmetical expression 10 + (12 – 4), first by using a single register (ie A); second by using two registers (ie A and B), leaving the results in register A.

First, using a single register:

```
MOV  A, 12        A = 12
SUB  A, 4         A = A – 4 = 12 – 4 = 8
ADD  A, 10        A = A + 10 = 8 + 10 = 18
```

Second, using two registers:

```
MOV  A,12         A = 12
MOV  B, 4         B = 4
SUB  A, B         A = A – B = 12 – 4 = 8
ADD  A, 10        A = A + 10 = 8 + 10 = 18
```

You might sometimes be asked to start your program with 'BEGIN' and finish with 'END', but this is considered decorative rather than a necessary operation, and in the following tests is not required.

Now try the following 10 exercises and see how many you can complete in 15 minutes using Table 3.1 as your guide for command operations.

1. Implement the following mathematical equations in assembly language using a single register A:

   I = 1
   I = I + 12
   J = 6
   K = I + J

2. Implement the following expressions into assembly language using registers A and B:

   I = 10
   K = I + 4
   C = '9'
   D = C – 'M'

3. Implement the following instruction in assembly language:
   X = 2
   If X – Y = 0 Then X = X + 1
   Otherwise Y = Y + 1

4. Write a program which causes a jump to an instruction labelled ZERO if the value of the variable COUNT is zero, or to an instruction labelled EQUAL if the value of the variable COUNT is equal to 100, or to an instruction labelled OTHER if the value of the variable COUNT is greater or less than 100.

5. Evaluate the following equation using two registers, A and B:

   (3 + 5) / (15 – 3) / (4 / 3) + (9 / 4) – (11 / 8) * X = 0

6. Write a program to evaluate the following expression using two registers A and B:

   {(11 – 2) / 3) X + (6 * 3 / 9) – I)}Y

7. Compare two variables stored in registers A and B. If they are equal then add 20 to A and subtract 5 from B. If they are not equal then add 2 to A and subtract 2 from B.

8. Multiply two numbers, NUM1 and NUM2, by 4 and put the results in R1 and R2 respectively, using registers A and B.

9. Write a program to sum sequences 2, 4, 6, 8, 10 up to 30. Store the results in a variable called TOTAL-SUM, using registers A and B.

10. Write a program to sum the integers 1 to 30 by an increment of 1 every time and store the result in a variable called SUM, using the single register B.

Spatial concepts

In this test you are often provided with the net of a benchmark unfolded box with a different pattern on each side. Your task is to build a three-dimensional image of the box. Then you have to compare the box from different angles and views with a set of boxes, decide which of these boxes matches the benchmark box, and mark your answer. Of course, you have to twist and turn the box in different directions in order to be able to visualize the whole pattern. In this book I have presented four methods of visualization of the three-dimensional box by twisting and rotating the sides around the two identified bases as shown in Figures 3.1, 3.2, 3.3 and 3.4 and their solutions. The dotted line indicates the formation of the box around the two bases from two different angles sufficient to visualize the shape of the box. Study all the diagrams carefully; copy one or all of the given diagrams and try to build a box and see how the patterns are arranged from different angles. Remember, a box always has six sides, no matter what.

TIPS

- First identify the two bases (B) of the unfolded box and always use them as a benchmark to compare and view the other given boxes. Then follow one of the four methods presented in this book to build up the three-dimensional box. Twisting and rotating the sides by 90, 180 and 360 degrees towards the two identified bases will show you how the box will look if it is folded from different angles. In this way you will able to visualize how the pattern on each side is adjusted in relation to a different base from different angles.
- I recommend that in your test you spend a couple of seconds drawing a very quick and simple draft of what the shape of the folded box would look like from the view angle of the two bases before you start answering the questions. In this way you will be assured that your answers will be correct, and it will save time and avoid unnecessary confusion.
- Different sizes and shapes of boxes may be used, eg rectangular for all sides, two sides wider than the other four sides, etc. The methods used in this book always hold; try it and see for yourself. Again, identify the bases and then rotate the sides towards each base to form three-dimensional shapes from different angles.

Figure 3.1 Net

Figure 3.1 Three-dimensional solution

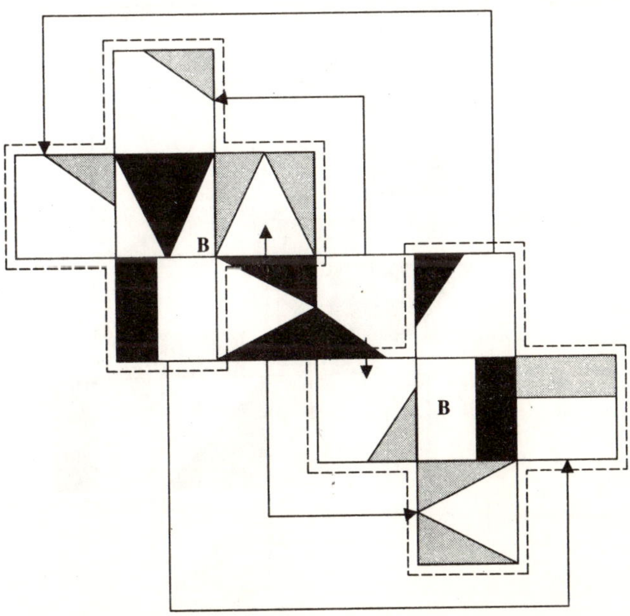

Figure 3.2 Net

Figure 3.2 Three-dimensional solution

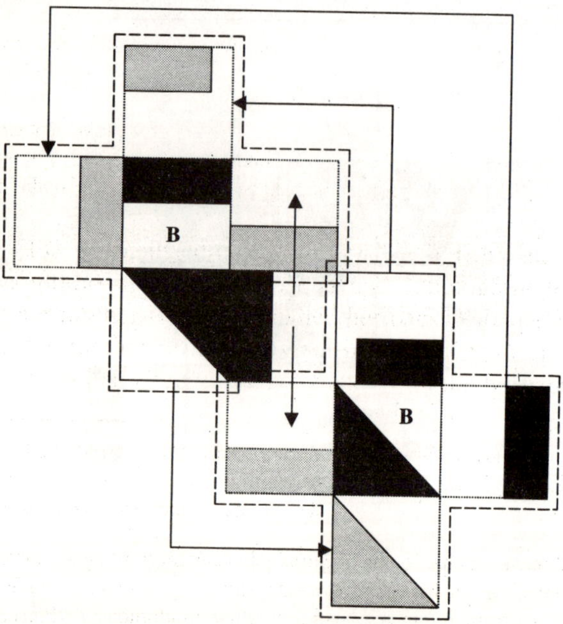

Figure 3.3 Net

Figure 3.3 Three-dimensional solution

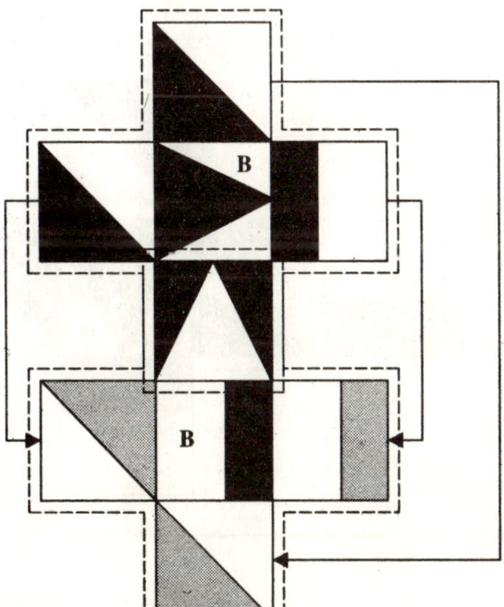

Figure 3.4 Net

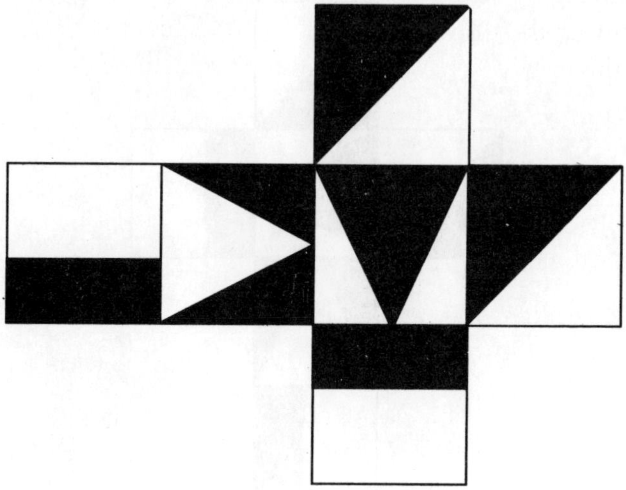

Figure 3.4 Three-dimensional solution

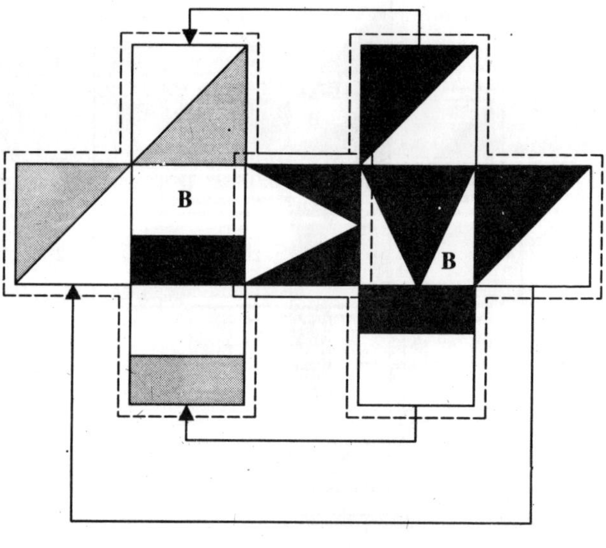

Now, look at Figure 3.5 and see how many of the associated questions in Figure 3.6 you can complete in 3 minutes. Compare your results with the answers given at the end of this chapter. To help you with this exercise I have provided the three-dimensional solution.

Figure 3.5 Net

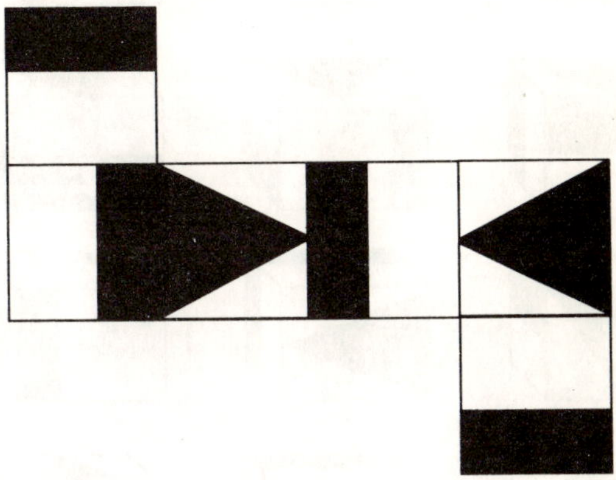

Figure 3.5 Three-dimensional solution

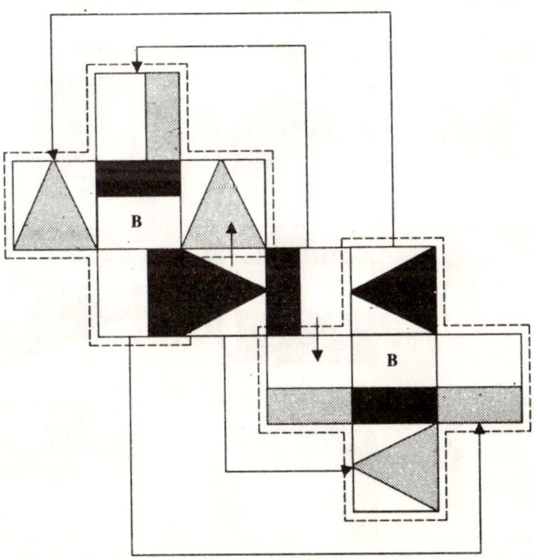

Figure 3.6

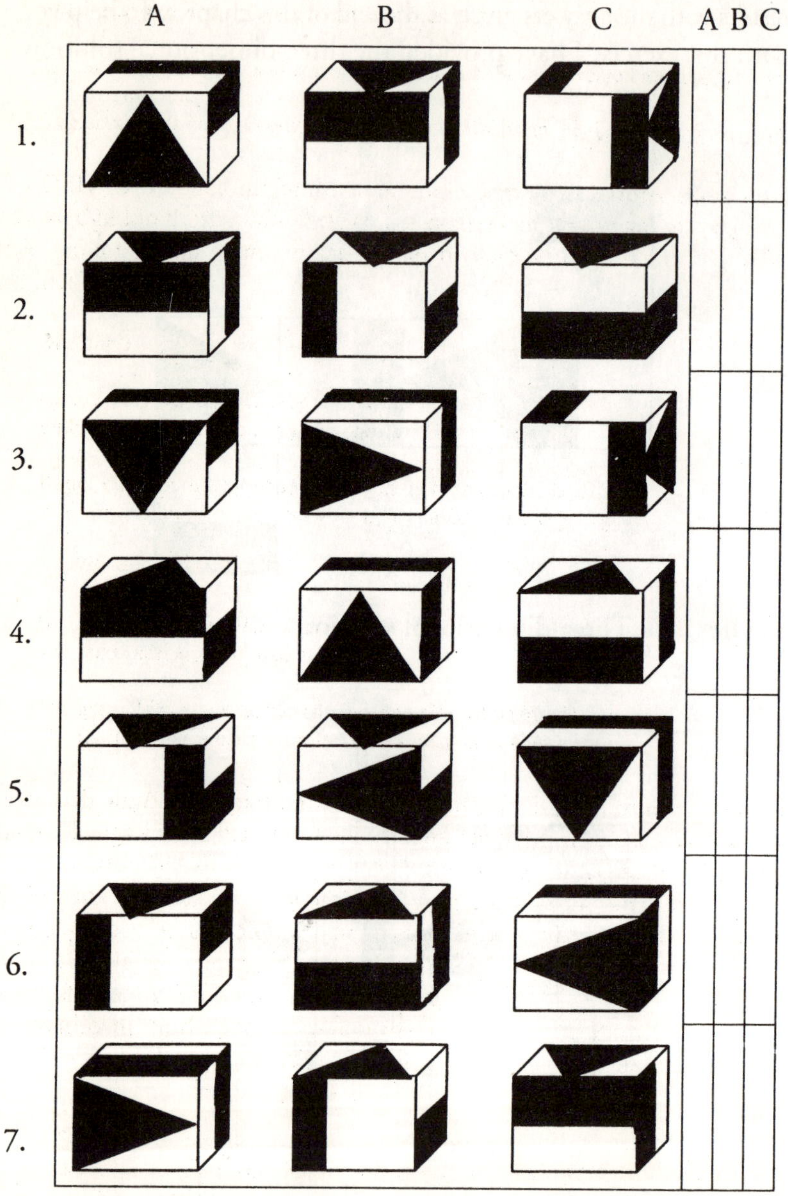

A B C

8.
9.
10.
11.
12.
13.
14.

A B C

Answers to Chapter 3

Compiler checking by tracking error (page 49)

1. SE
2. NE
3. OE
4. SE, LE
5. SE
6. OE
7. LE
8. SE
9. SE, OE
10. SE, OE
11. SE, OE
12. NE
13. SE
14. NE
15. SE, LE
16. NE
17. SE
18. LE
19. SE, LE
20. SE, OE
21. SE, LE, OE
22. SE, LE
23. OE
24. SE, OE
25. NE
26. SE, LE
27. SE, LE, OE
28. OE
29. LE
30. SE, LE
31. NE
32. NE
33. OE
34. SE
35. SE, OE
36. SE, OE
37. NE
38. LE
39. NE
40. NE
41. LE, OE

Compiler checking by line rules (page 52)

1. Z
2. Y
3. X, Y
4. X
5. Y
6. X, Y

7. Z
8. W
9. W
10. W, Y
11. X,Y
12. Y
13. Z
14. X, Y
15. Z
16. W
17. Z
18. Z
19. X, Y
20. W, Y
21. W, X
22. W
23. Y
24. Z
25. W
26. Z
27. W, X
28. W, X, Y
29. W
30. Z
31. Z
32. W
33. W
34. W
35. Z
36. W
37. X, Y
38. X
39. W
40. Y

Assembly language test (page 60)

1.
```
MOV   I, 1          I = 1
ADD   I, 12         I = I + 12
MOV   J, 6          J = 6
MOV   A, J          A = J
ADD   A, I          A = I + J
MOV   K, A          K = A = I + J
```

2.
```
MOV   I, 10         I = 10
ADD   I, 4          I = I + 4
MOV   A, I          A = I, A = I + 4
MOV   K, A          K = A = I + 4
MOV   C, '9'        C = '9'
SUB   C, 'M'        C = C – 'M'
```

MOV	B, C	B = C
MOV	D, B	D = B = C – 'M'

3. MOV	X, 2	X = 2
SUB	X, Y	X = X – Y = 2 – Y
JMPZ	Next	If X – Y = 0 then jump to N Next
INC	Y	If X – Y not equal to 0 then Y = Y + 1
Next:	INC	X X = X + 1

4. MOV	A, COUNT	A = COUNT
JMPZ	ZERO	If COUNT = 0, go to ZERO
CMP	100	Compare COUNT with 100
JMPE	EQUAL	If COUNT = 100 then go to EQUAL
JMP	OTHER	Otherwise go to OTHER
ZERO:		
EQUAL:		
OTHER:		

5. After simplifying algebraic expressions you get

$$22 - 11X = 0$$

MOV	B, 11	B = 11
MUL	B, X	B = 11X
MOV	A, 22	A = 22
SUB	A, B	A = A – B = 22 – 11X
MOV	A, 0	A = 22 – 11X = 0

6. After simplifying algebraic expressions you get

{3X + (2 – I)} Y

```
        MOV   A, 2          A = 2
        SUB   A, I          A = 2 – I
        MOV   B, 3          B = 3
        MUL   B, X          B = 3X
        ADD   B, A          B = B + A = 3X + 2 – I
        MUL   B, Y          B = {3X + (2 – I)}Y
```

7.

```
        CMP   A, B          Compare the contents of
                            A and B
        JMPZ  Both-Equal    If A = B then go to
                            Both-Equal

                            Otherwise
        ADD   A, 2          A = A + 2;
        SUB   B, 2          B = B – 2;
        JMP   Endfile       go to Endfile, used to
                            declare end not essential
Both-Equal:                 Here A = B
        ADD   A, 20
        SUB   B, 5
Endfile:
```

8.

```
        MOV   A, NUM1       A = NUM1
        ADD   A, A          A = A * 2 = A + A
        ADD   A, A          A = (A * 2) * 2 =
                            (A + A) + (A + A) = 4A
        MOV   R1, A         R1 = 4A
        MOV   B, NUM2       B = NUM2
        ADD   B, B
        ADD   B, B          B = 4B
        MOV   R2, B         R2 = AB
```

9.	MOV	A, TOTAL-SUM	A = TOTAL-SUM
	MUL	A, 0	A = TOTAL-SUM = 0
	MOV	B, 2	Set the counter, B = 2
Repeat:	CMP	B, 30	Is B = 30?
	JMPE	Finish	Go to Finish if B = 30, Otherwise
	ADD	TOTAL-SUM, B	TOTAL-SUM = 0 + 2 = 2
	ADD	B, 2	B = B + 2 = 2 + 2 = 4
	JMP	Repeat	Continue adding until you reach 30
Finish:			

10.	MOV	SUM, 0	SUM = 0
	MOV	B, 1	Set the counter, B = 1
Repeat:	CMP	B, 30	
	JMPE	Finish	
	ADD	SUM, B	SUM = SUM + B = 0 + 1
	INC	B	B = B + 1 = 1 + 1 = 2
	JMP	Repeat	
Finish:			

Spatial concepts (page 68)

1. A
2. C
3. B
4. C
5. C
6. B
7. C
8. A
9. A
10. C
11. C
12. A
13. C
14. C

4

Common Numerical Psychometric Tests

Introduction

In common with the employment procedures of other industries, all candidates applying for IT, finance and management jobs have to take a numerical test, to test their abilities to work with numbers. In this book I present three kinds of test which are widely used and which deal with basic principles of arithmetic (addition, subtraction, multiplication and division). Knowledge of mathematical terminology, symbols and processes such as percentage, ratio, roots, decimals, fractions, powers and exponents is usually required. Therefore, brush up your maths skills and consult your old maths books because the basics are not covered here. The first and second sections of this chapter deal with estimation calculation and problem solving worked out without the use of a calculator. However, in section 3, which deals with the interpretation of tables and graphs, you are free to use one. I urge you throughout this chapter to look at the given answer choice before working on the problem, to give you an idea of what you should expect and help you to exclude unreasonable alternatives.

Numerical estimation

In this test you are presented with a variety of questions to which you must estimate the answer. Quick mental arithmetic can be done using scrap paper. However, in a real test you would have no time. Therefore try to practise and familiarize yourself with these types of problem. Always keep in mind that you are never asked to supply an exact answer for the question; you are only asked to estimate which of the given choices is closest.

TIPS

To give you practice in avoiding common mistakes:

- If you have to multiply/divide and add/subtract, do the multiplication/division first as in this example:

  20 – 5 + 9 * 5 ÷ 5 = 20 – 5 + 45 ÷ 5 = 20 – 5 + 9 = 24

- If you have to divide and multiply by the same number, then don't bother; the result is always 1 as shown below:

  (10 ÷ 5) 5 = 10 or 20 + 5 * 15 ÷ 15 = 25

- Use quick mental arithmetic, for example:

292 + 398 + 102 + 801	A	B	C	D
	1,598	1,593	1,590	1,597

  The quick mental arithmetic 300 + 400 +100 + 800 gives a result of 1600, therefore all the suggested answers A, B, C, D appear possible at first. However, if you add the remaining unit numbers you get –8 – 2 + 2 + 1 = –7. So only B can be the right answer, since 1,600 – 7 = 1,593.
- Allocate your time effectively and leave the difficult questions for later to sort out if you still have time left.

Now try the test below in Table 4.1, which consists of 30 questions that must be answered within a time limit of 7 minutes. The questions range from very easy to quite challenging.

Table 4.1

		A	B	C	D
1.	304 ÷ 2 + 15 – 25 = ?	138	142	135	145
2.	4 + 6 * 2 ÷ 2 * 1 + 3 – 5 = ?	8	6	5	10
3.	9 1/4 + 10 ¾ – 2 3/2 + 2.5 = ?	18	17	19	21
4.	6 2/4 ÷ ½ * 4/2 = ?	7.5	7	6	6.5
5.	9/3 * 75/5 ÷ 4/12 * 48/2 + 5/10 * 20/4 – 5 = ?	4	3	5	6
6.	1/2 + 2/6 + 7/4 + 9/2 – 8/2 = ?	6	4	3	5
7.	7 + 6.241 + 18.021 + 2.2 = ?	29	30	35	33
8.	8.1 + 2.33 + 9.001 + 16.02 = ?	35	37	33	31
9.	5.020 – 1.112 – 1.021 – 0.38 = ?	2.8	2.5	2.9	2.7
10.	(7.5 + 55) / (0.05) + 10 = ?	1270	1255	1260	1250
11.	(82 – 0.44) / (2.002) + 15 = ?	54	56	58	59
12.	20% + 15% + 65% + 1 = ?	2	1	3	1.5
13.	13% * 2/65 + 10 = ?	9.5	10.5	11	10
14.	50% * 120/50 + 300/100 + 100% – 2 = ?	3.8	3	4	4.5
15.	7 + 58 + (–4) + 8 – (–5) = ?	74	73	75	72
16.	–2 + (–6.2) – (–0.2) – (–5) = ?	+3	–4	+4	–3
17.	–5.8 + 3 + (–2.18) – (–10.06) + (–1.08) = ?	–4	4	3.5	-3.5
18.	–10 + 19 – (–2) + (–3) + (+2) = ?	10.5	9	10	11

Table 4.1 Continued

		A	B	C	D
19.	(–3) (+2) + (–10) (–2) – (+2) (+4) = ?	6	–2	5	–3
20.	(–9) (–2) + (–8) (–6) – (–5) (–4) = ?	–46	46	–12	40
21.	5426 – 3202 + 236 – 980 = ?	–1480	1485	1475	1480
22.	9302 + 2105 – 9003 + 12 = ?	2419	–2420	2416	2418
23.	120 ½ + 180 ¾ – 50 1/5 – 2 4/5 = ?	248	245	249	250
24.	12 2/5 – 19 ¾ + 6 6/5 + 3 3/2 = ?	4 7/25	4 9/20	4 5/18	4 7/20
25.	–23 + 73 9/6 +19 – 22 5/4 = ?	49	47 9/6	46 5/4	52
26.	$\sqrt{25} + \sqrt{36} - \sqrt{144}$ = ?	13	+1	–1	0
27.	$3\sqrt{25} + 3\sqrt{9} - 5\sqrt{49}$ = ?	–11	10	–35	15
28.	$2\sqrt{36} - 10\sqrt{9} + 3\sqrt{25} - 2\sqrt{49}$ = ?	17	–17	15	–15
29.	$8^{1/3} + 25^{1/2} + 9^{1/2} - 2$ = ?	10	9	7	8
30.	$27^{1/3} + 125^{1/3} - 512^{1/3}$ = ?	3	0	–1	1

Problem solving

This test requires, as well as a knowledge of mathematical principles, an understanding of the fundamentals of algebra and arithmetic.

TIP

As they say, understanding the question is half the answer. Therefore read carefully and make sure you know what is required of you. Avoid making assumptions about costs rising, etc. Use only the information given in the question. Try quick mental arithmetic if possible. Also practise the mathematical operations presented in the previous section as well as others such as averages, fractions etc which are useful for this section, before you start the test. Nearly all of the questions are easily answered once you have figured out how the question works. Don't perform unnecessary calculations if you can use quick mental calculations. The time you save can be used to check other questions.

The following test will give you the necessary confidence for the real test in order to avoid unnecessary mistakes.

Now try the test below, which consists of 21 questions that must be answered within a time limit of 9 minutes.

1. How much will it cost to build a wall round a house that is 25 metres long and 75 metres wide, if the cost of 50 cm is £10?

A	B	C
£4,000	£40,000	£400

2. It costs a publisher *n* pounds for each book to publish the first 1,000 books; extra books cost *n*/6 pounds each. How many pounds will it cost to publish 7,000 books?

A	B	C
7,000*n*	2,000*n*	5,000

3. The distance between London and Hull is 300 miles. An Intercity train travels at 120 miles per hour from London to Hull. The train then goes back to London. If the total journey time was 4 hours and 30 minutes, what was the average speed of the Intercity train on the way back to London?

A	B	C
160 mph	140 mph	150 mph

4. At weekends the local Bowling club charges each person a flat rate of *n* pounds for up to 3 hours and 1/9*n* for each hour or fraction of an hour after the first 3 hours. How much does it cost for 2 people to go for 6 hours and 25 minutes at the weekend?

A	B	C
6/9n	26/9*n*	13/9*n*

5. John bought £3,000 worth of stocks in company X. He sold 2/3 of his stock after the value doubled, then sold the remaining stock at 4 times its purchase price. What was the total profit on the stock of company X?

A	B	C
£3,000	£4,000	£5,000

6. The price of a barrel of oil in 1998, 1999 and 2000 rose 10 per cent more over the previous year's price. How much more did the consumer have to pay in 2000 than in 1998?

A	B	C
19%	21%	23%

7. Assume that British Airways own 40% of the stock in Virgin Atlantic company. Easyjet own 20,000 shares in Virgin. Midland own all the shares not owned by British Airways or Easyjet. How many shares does British Airways own if Midland has 25% more shares than British Airways?

A	B	C
80,000	75,000	100,000

8. A market research exercise in England of n young people under 15 years found that 30 per cent liked McDonald's. An additional x young people were asked and all of them liked McDonald's. Eighty per cent of all the young people who took part in the market research claimed they liked McDonald's. Find n young people in terms of x.

A	B	C
3.5	2.5n	3

9. Peter, David and Tina ate lunch together. Tina's bill was 70 per cent more than David's bill. Peter's bill was 11/9 as much as Tina's bill. If David paid £10 for his lunch, approximately how much was the total bill that the three paid?

A	B	C
£48	£52	£45

10. A surveyor assessed the value of a house in the north of England at £85,000. The assessed value represented only 50 per cent of the market value of the house. If Inland Revenue taxes are £5 for every £1,000 of the market value of the house, how much are the total taxes on the house?

A	B	C
£800	£637.5	£850

11. A ton of potatoes costs £20 and a ton of onions costs £29. If the price of potatoes rises by 15 per cent a month and the price of onions remains unchanged, how many months will it take before a ton of onions costs less than a ton of potatoes?

A	B	C
4	2	3

12. At one of the Save the Children Fund's charity banquets for wealthy people, 30 per cent of the guests contributed £60 each, 55 per cent contributed £15 each and the rest contributed £5 each. Approximately what percentage of the total banquet takings came from people who gave £15?

A	B	C
31%	42%	26%

13. A microwave oven originally cost £200. Before Christmas the oven was on sale at 110 per cent of its original cost. After the New Year when the sale season started, the oven was discounted 15 per cent and was sold. The oven was sold for what cost?

A	B	C
£253	£187	£220

14. There are 20 postmen in Crawley responsible for delivering mail. If a typical postman can deliver 30/2 pieces of mail in 30 minutes, how many pieces of mail should all postmen in Crawley be able to deliver in 3½ hours?

A	B	C
2,100	1,050	2,200

15. Butter costs 1/2 as much as cheese. Cheese costs 9/8 as much as milk. Milk costs what fraction of the cost of butter?

A	B	C
9/8	9/16	16/9

16. The total cost of typing a PhD thesis is £50. Merry typed 60 per cent of the thesis and Lina typed the rest. How much did Lina receive?

A	B	C
£20	£25	£30

17. A milkman delivered *x* bottles of milk on Monday, on Tuesday he delivered 3 times as many, and on Wednesday he delivered 120 bottles. Over the 3 days the milkman delivered 240 bottles. How many did he deliver on Tuesday?

A	B	C
30	90	120

18. An estate agent rented a house for £500 per month. Ten years later the tenant calculated that if he had bought the house and had a £200 per month mortgage he would have owned the house. How much would he have saved if he had bought the house?

A	B	C
£30,000	£24,000	£36,000

19. A team exploring the Amazon consists of 30 scientists; 1/3 are women, 2/3 are men. To obtain a team with 40 per cent women, how many men should be replaced by women?

A	B	C
2	5	8

20. An ice cream machine produces 6,000 lollies per hour. Because of maintenance the ice cream machine is not operational for 22 minutes. How many lollies are not produced because of maintenance?

A	B	C
2,225	2,200	2,275

21. The following are car production figures for plant A in a week: on Monday 200 cars, on Tuesday 300 cars, on Wednesday 400 cars, on Thursday 650 cars, on Friday 210 cars. What was the average car production for the week for plant A?

A	B	C
350	300	352

Interpretation of graphs and data

To be able to calculate and measure statistical information is very important for jobs in IT, finance and management.

TIPS

- Scan the whole graph or table before you start answering the questions.
- Carefully read the units, eg cm, m, pound, pennies etc, and make sure that you answer in the correct unit.

- As before, read the choices before you answer, because many questions need a little calculation and more intelligent reading to understand.
- A common mistake is mixing between decimals and percentages as shown in the example below:

  1/100 = 1% = 0.01
  10/100 = 10% = 0.1

- Always use your common sense to see if the answer makes sense.

Now work through the examples below and see how many you can finish in 25 minutes.

Figure 4.1 Continuous growth of sales and staff

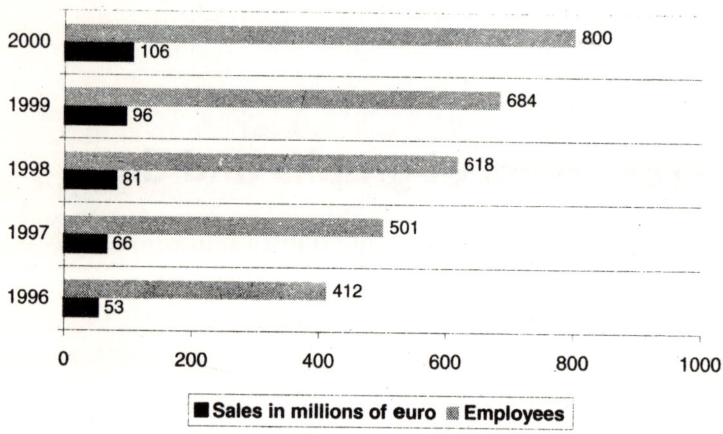

1. By approximately what percentage did total staff numbers change from year 1996 to 2000?

A	B	C
387	94%	90%

2. By what percentage did the total profit change from 1996 to 2000?

A	B	C
100%	53 million euro	50%

3. If the number of employees in 2001 has increased by 25 per cent over 2000, what was the total number of new recruits in 2001 compared with 2000?

A	B	C
200	1,000	1,200

4. Between 1996 and 2000, which years showed the smallest and largest staff profit numbers, respectively?

A	B	C
1996 and 2000	1999 and 1996	1999 and 1998

5. If 1 euro = £0.65, then the profit in 1999 was approximately

A	B	C
£6,240,000	£62.4 million	624,000,000 euro

6. If there are 300 additional recruits in 2001 and the average growth of sales and staff remains constant, how much greater would the total sales volume (in euro) for 2001 be?

A	B	C
£39.75 million	3,975,000 euro	39,750,000 euro

Figure 4.2 One week's temperatures in three capitals

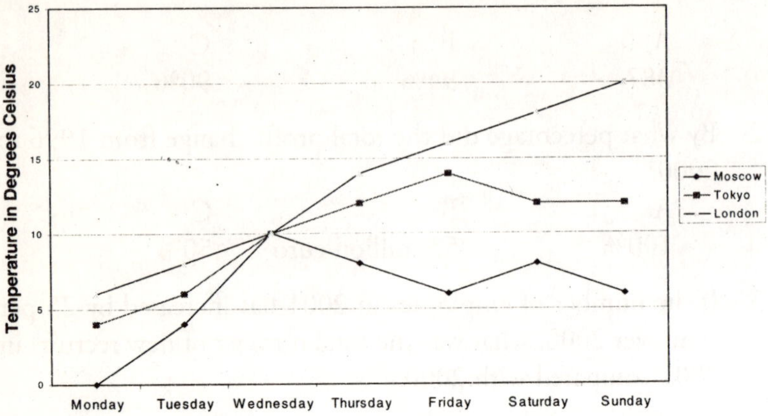

1. On which day did the three capitals have the same temperature?

A	B	C
Monday	Wednesday	Friday

2. Which day showed the largest increase in temperature in Moscow?

A	B	C
Wednesday	Saturday	Monday

3. In which capital was the trend of temperature consistent throughout the week?

A	B	C
London	Moscow	Tokyo

4. What was the average temperature for the week in Moscow?

A	B	C
8°	5.5°	6°

5. What was the average temperature for the week in Tokyo?

A	B	C
7°	8°	10°

6. What was approximately the percentage increase in temperature between Monday and Sunday in London?

A	B	C
237%	233%	245%

7. What was the ratio of the temperature in London on Sunday to the temperature in Moscow on Tuesday?

A	B	C
5:1	1:5	4:20

Figure 4.3 Income and expenditure for average family between 1990 and 2000

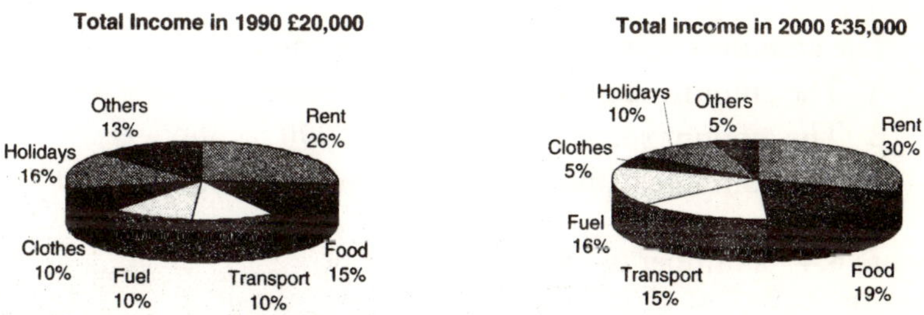

1. The yearly expenditure on holidays in 1990 was 160 per cent of the amount spent on:

A Transport in 1990
B Food in 1990
C Clothes in 2000

2. If the average family income in 2001 rises by 25 per cent over 2000 (and all percentage expenditures remain the same), how much will the average family spend on holidays in 2001?

   A £3,650
   B £3,500
   C £4,375

3. The combined expenditure in 1990 for transport, fuel and others was approximately the same as

   A 2/3 the amount spent on rent in 1990
   B The amount spent on food in 2000
   C The amount spent on clothes and others in 2000

4. The combined average family expenditure in 2000 for fuel, food, clothes and holidays was what fraction of the annual income?

   A 2/3
   B 1/2
   C 1/2

5. The amount spent on fuel in 2000 was the same as

   A The amount spent on transport in 1990
   B The amount spent on holidays in 1990
   C The combined amount spent on food and others in 1990

Figure 4.4 Number of cars sold in Europe

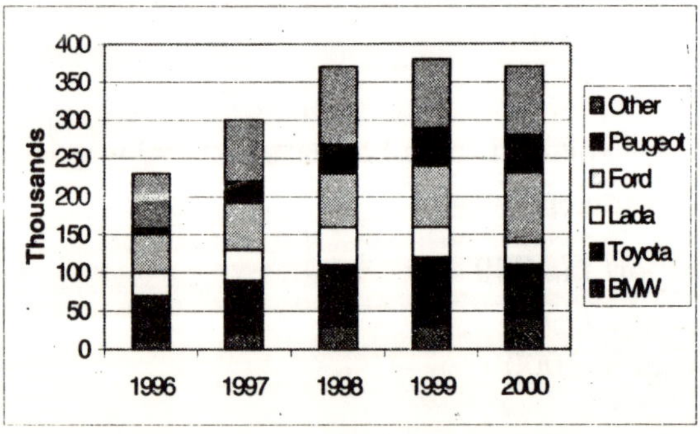

1. Approximately what percentage of cars sold in 2000 were Ford?

A	B	C
24%	30%	29%

2. From 1996 to 2000, of all the cars sold in Europe, the largest number of cars belonged to which manufacturer?

A	B	C
Ford	Peugeot	Toyota

3. Which car sales showed the most consistent increase between 1996 and 2000?

A	B	C
Lada	Ford	Peugeot

4. What was the average yearly number of cars sold by Toyota between 1996 and 2000?

A	B	C
74,000	7 million	82,000

5. Between 1996 and 2000, Peugeot car sales increased by what percentage?

A	B	C
50%	400%	40%

6. Which year showed the largest increase in other car sales over total car sales between 1996 and 2000?

A	B	C
2000	1999	1998

Table 4.2 Numbers of undergraduates, postgraduates and graduates of five universities between 1998 and 2000

University	1998 in thousands			1999 in thousands			2000 in thousands		
	Under-graduates	Post-graduates	Graduates	Under-graduates	Post-graduates	Graduates	Under-graduates	Post-graduates	Graduates
AAA	10	2	2	12	1.5	2.5	13	1	3
BBB	15	4	3	14	3	3	12	2	2.5
CCC	20	4	5	22	4.1	5.2	23	4.2	5.5
DDD	18	2	2.5	19	1.5	3	21	1	3.1
EEE	22	1	4	23	0.5	4.1	25	0.5	4.2

1. Which university has shown a decline in undergraduate numbers every year over the period 1998–2000?

A	B	C
AAA	BBB	EEE

2. What was the percentage increase in the total undergraduate numbers in all five universities in 2000 as compared with 1998 (to the nearest 4%)?

A	B	C
7%	9%	11%

3. Which universities had the same number of postgraduates and graduates between 1998 and 2000?

A	B	C
AAA and BBB	BBB and DDD	CCC and EEE

4. If in 2001 the number of undergraduate and postgraduate students in university EEE increased by 25% and 200% respectively over 2000, and the number of graduates remained the same, what approximately was the total number of undergraduates, postgraduates and graduates in university EEE in 2001?

A	B	C
369,500	0.3695 million	36,950

Table 4.3 Sales volume in five mobile phone companies over the last four years, in thousands

Company	1996	1997	1998	1999	2000
Nokia	580	679	887	998	1,187
Ericsson	294	493	548	598	632
Orange	192	232	268	312	366
Cellnet	120	209	204	302	366
BT	403	399	562	593	821

1. Which mobile phone companies have shown a decline in sales over the period 1996–2000?

A	B	C
Cellnet and BT	BT and Nokia	Ericsson and Cellnet

2. Of all these mobile phone companies, which showed a proportional increase in sales between 1999 and 2000, and which showed the smallest and the largest increase as compared to 1999?

A	B	C
Cellnet and Ericsson	Ericsson and BT	BT and Orange

3. For all companies combined, what is the percentage increase in sales between 1999 and 1998 (to the nearest 4%)?

A	B	C
11%	14%	12%

4. What is the average sales for Ericsson from 1996 to 2000?

A	B	C
0.05135 million	513,000	512,000

5. Which mobile company's sales volume in 2000 was approximately three times its sales in 1996?

A	B	C
Ericsson	Nokia	Cellnet

6. Which mobile company had the lowest increase in sales volume in 2000 as compared with 1997?

A	B	C
Orange	Ericsson	Nokia

Table 4.4 EU members' statistical information in 2000

Country	Population in millions	Total employment in millions	% below the poverty line	% unemployed women to total unemployment	Total employment: unemployment
Portugal	10	5	29	49.5	2:1
Greece	12	6	24	57.5	5:2
UK	58	20	16	35.1	10:2
Spain	38	19	19	60.8	3:2
Italy	48	20	18	52.2	12:3
France	60	25	16	54.7	10:3
Netherlands	11	5.5	14	47.7	4:2
Belgium	13	5	13	30.5	8:3
Germany	68	34	13	58.5	9:3

1. Which country had the highest number of people below the poverty line in 2000?

A	B	C
France	UK	Spain

2. What was the total number of unemployed men in Italy in 2000, in millions?

A	B	C
2.29	2.39	2.61

3. The total number of unemployed women in 2000 was about x million in Belgium, with x equal to about

A	B	C
2.43	0.57	1.3

4. If in 2000 unemployed women aged 60 or over made up only 1/3 of the total unemployed women in Greece, how many men aged 60 or over were unemployed?

A	B	C
Can't say	1.38 million	0.46 million

5. The ratio of population in 2000 between France and Portugal was?

A	B	C
10:60	1:6	6:1

6. Which countries had the highest and lowest number of unemployed men in 2000?

A	B	C
Spain and Greece	Germany and Portugal	Germany and Greece

Answers to Chapter 4

Numerical estimation (page 77)

1. B
2. A
3. C
4. D
5. B
6. C
7. D
8. A
9. B
10. C
11. B
12. A
13. D
14. B
15. A
16. D
17. B
18. C
19. A
20. B
21. D
22. C
23. A
24. D
25. C
26. C
27. A
28. B
29. D
30. B

Problem solving (page 79)

1. A
2. B
3. C
4. B
5. C
6. B
7. A
8. B
9. A
10. C
11. C
12. A
13. B
14. A
15. C
16. A
17. B
18. C
19. A
20. B
21. C

Interpretation of graphs and data (page 84)

Figure 4.1 Continuous growth of sales and staff

1. B
2. A
3. A
4. B
5. B
6. C

Figure 4.2 One week's temperatures in three capitals

1. B
2. A
3. A
4. C
5. C
6. B
7. A

Figure 4.3 Income and expenditure for average family between 1990 and 2000

1. A
2. C
3. B
4. B
5. C

Figure 4.4 Number of cars sold in Europe

1. A
2. C
3. B
4. A
5. B
6. C

Table 4.2 Numbers of undergraduates, postgraduates and graduates of five universities between 1998 and 2000

1. B
2. C
3. A
4. C

Table 4.3 Sales volume in five mobile phone companies over the last four years, in thousands

1. A
2. B
3. B
4. B
5. C
6. A

Table 4.4 EU members' statistical information in 2000

1. A
2. B
3. B
4. A
5. C
6. A

Tips on solving the problems in problem solving

1. The perimeter of the house is 25 + 25 + 75 + 75 = 200. The total cost = £10 * 200/0.5 = £400, therefore A is correct.

2. The first 1,000 books cost *n* pounds for each book, so altogether they will cost 1,000*n*. The total cost is 1,000*n* + 6,000**n*/6 = 2,000*n*, therefore B is correct.

3. Distance = Speed * Time.
   300 = 120 * Time; Time = 2.5 hours from London to Hull.
   Total journey took 4 hours 30 minutes, so the time taken from Hull to London is 5.5 – 2.5 = 2 hours.
   Speed = 300/2 = 150 mph, therefore C is correct.

4. For 1 person it cost = *n* + 1/9 * 4*n* = 13/9*n*. For 2 persons, multiply by two, therefore B is correct.

5. John sold his stock at = 2/3 * £3,000 = £2,000.
   Value was doubled = 2 * £2,000 = £4,000; and he made a profit of £4,000 – £2,000 = £2,000.
   The remaining stock, £3,000 – £2,000 = £1,000, was sold at £1,000 * 4 = £4,000 and the profit he made was £4,000 – £1,000 = £3,000. The total profit was £2,000 + £3,000 = £5,000, therefore C is the correct answer.

6. Let X denote the price in 1998. In 1999 the price rose to 110% of X which is (1.1) X, and in 2000 the price rose to 110% of (1.1)X which is (1.1)(1.1)X or 1.21 X. Therefore the price of oil rose by 21% more in 2000.

7. If Midland owns 25% more than British Airways and British Airways own 40% of Virgin Atlantic, then Midland must own 1.25 * 0.4 = 50% of Virgin Atlantic, since Easyjet = 100% – 40% – 50% = 10%.
   If 10% of the shares in Virgin Atlantic is 20,000 shares, then there must be 200,000 shares in Virgin Atlantic. British Airways' shares are 200,000 * 0.4 = 80,000, so that A is the correct answer.

8. The total number of people researched is $0.3n + x = 0.8(n + x)$.
   $x = 2.5n$, so B is the correct answer.

9. Tina = 1.7. David and Peter = 11/9 Tina, so Peter = 11/9 * 1.7 David = 2 David.
   David paid £10 for his lunch, therefore Peter paid £20 and Tina paid £17, and the total bill for the three of them was approximately £48.

10. First find the market value of the house, which means £85,000/0.5= £170,000. The tax rate is £5 for every £1,000, or 0.005. Therefore the total tax is 0.005 * £170,000 = £850.

11. The price of potatoes will be £20 $(1.15)^n$. After n months the price must be greater than £29, ie when $(1.15)^n$ is greater than £29/£20 = 1.45. Since 1.15 * 1.15 = 1.32 and 1.15 * 1.15 * 1.15 = 1.52, after three months the cost of a ton of onions will be less than the cost of a ton of potatoes.

12. Assume 100 people were invited. Therefore 30% represents 30 persons, who contributed £60, 55% represents 55 persons, who contributed £15, and the rest represent 15% or 15 persons who contributed £5. The total amount of contribution is £2,700, and the percentage of the total banquet takings coming from people who gave £15 = 825/£2,700 = 31%, therefore answer A is correct.

13. Since 110% of £200 = £220, the microwave oven was offered for sale at £220 before Christmas. It was sold for (100% – 15%) = 85% of £220, since there was a 15% discount. Therefore the oven was sold for 0.85 * £220 = £187.

14. Since 30 minutes is half of one hour, in 3.5 hours the postmen should deliver 20 * 7 * 30/2 = 2,100 pieces of mail.

15. Butter = 1/2 Cheese, and Cheese = 9/8 Milk. Therefore Butter = 1/2 * 9/8 Milk, and Milk's cost as a fraction of Butter is Milk/Butter = 16/9.

16. Merry typed 60% * £50 = 30, therefore Lina typed £20 worth of the PhD thesis.

17. Assume that on Monday the milkman delivered x bottles of milk, on Tuesday he delivered 3x and on Wednesday he delivered 120. The total is x + 3x + 120 = 240, therefore x = 30, and on Tuesday he delivered 3x = 3 * 30 = 90 bottles of milk.

18. Rent on the house for 10 years is £500 * 10 * 12 = £60,000. If the tenant had bought the house the mortgage would have

been £200 * 10 * 12 = £24,000. Therefore he would have saved £36,000.

19. We have 10 women and 20 men in the team. To obtain 40% women, 40% * 30 = 12. We already have 10, so we need another 2. The answer is A.

20. Number of lollies per minute = 6,000/60 = 100. We have 22 minutes * 100 = 2,200.

21. The average = (200 + 300 + 400 + 650 + 210) / 5 = 352.

Tips on solving the problems in interpretation of graphs and data

Figure 4.1 Continuous growth of sales and staff

1. In 1996 the total staff number was 412 and in 2000 it was 800. Therefore the total staff increase between 1996 and 2000, expressed as a percentage, is (800 – 412)/412 * 100 = 94.17% »94%.

2. The total profit changes between 1996 and 2000, expressed as a percentage, is
(106 – 53)/53 * 100 = 100%.

3. Number of employees in the year 2001 is 25% * 800 + 800 = 1,000, and the total number of new recruits in 2001 is 1,000 – 800 = 200.

4. The staff profit ratio for 1996: 412/53 = 7.77
1997: 501/66 = 7.59
1998: 618/81 = 7.62

1999: 684/96 = 7.125
2000: 800/106 = 7.54
Therefore in 1999 the staff profit ratio was the smallest, and in 1996 the largest.

5. If one euro is equivalent to £0.65, then profit in 1999 is 97 * 0.65 = £62.4 million.

6. Total number of employees in 2001: 800 + 300 = 1,100, since the average growth of sales and staff remains constant compared to 2000. Therefore the total sales is (106 * 1,100)/800 = 145.75 and this amount was greater than in 2000 by 145.75 – 106 = 39.75 million euro = 39,750,000 euro. Check the decimal number in multiple choices carefully to ensure that the number is in millions of euro.

Figure 4.2 One week's temperatures in three capitals

1. The answer is B, since all three capitals have the same temperature.

2. The answer is A; the line shows the largest increase in temperature for a week in Moscow.

3. Scanning the graph, it is clear that London shows a consistent increase in temperature from Monday to Sunday.

4. The average temperature for the week in Moscow is (0 + 4° + 10° + 8° + 6° + 8° + 6°)/7 = 6°.

5. The average temperature for a week in Tokyo is (4° + 6° + 10° + 12° + 14° + 12° + 12°)/7 = 10°.

6. The temperature in London on Monday was 6° and on Sunday 20°; the approximate percentage increase over a week is 20° – 6° / 6° * 100 = 233.33% ≈ 233%.

7. The temperature in London on Sunday was 20° and the temperature in Moscow on Tuesday was 4°. The ratio is 20°/4° = 5/1 = 5:1.

Figure 4.3 Income and expenditure for average family between 1990 and 2000

1. Here you will find the ratio of the percentages. In 1990, 16% of the expenditure was for holidays. We want *x* where 160% of *x* = 16%, so *x* = 10%. Any category that received 10% of 1990 expenditures gives the correct answer. By simply looking at the pie graph it is obvious that transport in 1990 is the correct answer.

2. The average family income in 2001: 25% * 35,000 + 35,000 = £43,750. If the percentage expenditure on holidays in 2001 is similar to 2000 and equals 10%, then the average family expenditure on holidays in 2001: £43,750 * 10% = £4,375.

3. By adding the percentages: transport, fuel and others in 1990 we get 10% + 10% + 13% = 33%, therefore the combined expenditure is 33% * £20,000 = £6,600. Now you have to compare this figure with the three relationships given as multiple choices in A: 3/2 * 26% * £20,000 = £346.66, which is not correct. Then B: 19% * £35,000 = £6,650. Finally C: 5% * £35,000 = £1,750, which is incorrect. Therefore B is the closest value and is the correct answer.

4. By adding all the expenditures: fuel, food, clothes and holidays we get 16% + 19% + 5% + 10% = 50% = 1/2, therefore B is the correct answer.

5. The amount spent on fuel in 2000 is 16% * 35,000 = £5,600. Now evaluate the given three multiple choices to find any equivalent:

A: 10% * 20,000 = £2,000
B: 16% * 20,000 = £3,200
C: 15% + 13% = 28% * 20,000 = £5,600, which is the correct answer.

Figure 4.4 Number of cars sold in Europe

To compare several categories using a graph of the cumulative type where the bar is divided up proportionately among different quantities needs careful evaluation of each quantity. To make the quantities clear to you and to help you to understand the graph, I have prepared below a simple table with all quantities.

	BMW	TOYOTA	LADA	FORD	PEUGEOT	OTHER
1996	10	60	30	50	10	70
1997	20	70	40	60	30	80
1998	30	80	50	70	40	100
1999	30	90	40	80	50	90
2000	40	70	30	90	50	90

1. Total cars sold in 2000 in thousands were 40 + 70 + 30 + 90 + 50 + 90 = 370 and the percentage of Ford cars sold in 2000 is 90/370 * 100 = 24.32% ≈ 24%.

2. To find which manufacturer sold the most cars, simply calculate the numbers of cars sold in thousands between 1996 and 2000 for the three models given in your multiple choices:

   Ford: 50 + 60 + 70 + 80 + 90 = 350
   Peugeot: 10 + 30 + 40 + 50 + 50 = 180
   Toyota: 60 + 70 + 80 + 90 + 70 = 370

   Therefore the largest number of cars sold in thousands between 1996 and 2000 was by Toyota.

3. By scanning all the quantities in the table above, it is clear that Ford had consistently increased its car sales between 1996 and 2000.

4. The average number of cars sold by Toyota between 1996 and 2000, in thousands: (60 + 70 + 80 + 90 + 70)/5 = 74. Make sure you know where the decimal point is and that the number is multiplied by thousands.

5. Peugeot car sales expressed as a percentage between 1996 and 2000, in thousands: (50 – 10)/10 * 100 = 400%.

6. Scanning the table above, you find that in 1998 other car sales were the largest between 1996 and 2000.

Table 4.2 Numbers of undergraduates, postgraduates and graduates of five universities between 1998 and 2000

1. Simply scanning the table may be the best strategy here. All you need to do is find only one of the three universities given in the multiple choices where the number of undergraduates declined between 1998 and 2000. Here University BBB shows a decline in undergraduates numbers every year over the period 1998–2000 and is the correct answer.

2. *Important note.* Carefully add all the figures in questions like this, otherwise the round number may be calculated differently and that may lead you to choose the wrong answer in multiple choices, which are deliberately designed with the options very near to each other.
   Total undergraduate number in thousands in all five universities in 1998 was 10 + 15 + 20 + 18 + 22 = 85.
   Total undergraduate number in thousands in all five universities in 2000 was 13 + 12 + 23 + 21 + 25 = 94.

The increase expressed as a percentage: (94 – 85)/85 * 100 = 10.58% = 11%.

3. Scanning the table carefully for all five universities, you will find that university AAA has 2,000 postgraduates and graduates in 1998 and university BBB has 3,000 postgraduates and graduates in 1999. No other university shows similar characteristics. Therefore AAA and BBB is the correct answer.

4. In 2001 the number of undergraduates in thousands in university EEE was 25% * 25 + 25 = 31,250.
The number of postgraduates in 2001 is 200% * 0.5 + 0.5 = 1,500 respectively. However, the number of graduates remains the same for 2001, so the total number is 4,200 + 31,250 + 1,500 = 36,950. Again check your decimal point carefully.

Table 4.3 Sales volume in five mobile phone companies over the last four years, in thousands

1. By scanning the table for all five mobile companies, you will find that Cellnet and BT have shown a decline in sales over the period 1996–2000.

2. All five mobile companies showed an increase in sales between 1999 and 2000. Nokia's increase was: 1,187 – 998 = 189, therefore the proportional increase was 189/998 = 0.189.
Ericsson's increase was: 632 – 598 = 34, therefore the proportional increase was 34/598 = 0.056.
Orange's increase was: 366 – 312 = 54, therefore the proportional increase was 54/312 = 0.173.
Cellnet's increase was: 366 – 302 = 64, therefore the proportional increase was 64/302 = 0.211.
BT's increase was: 821 – 593 = 228, therefore the proportional increase was 228/593 = 0.384.

Therefore the smallest proportional increase is 0.056 (for Ericsson) and the largest proportional increase is 0.384 (for BT).

3. The total sales in thousands for all mobile companies in 1998 was 887 + 548 + 268 + 204 + 562 = 2,469 and in 1999 it was 998 + 598 + 312 + 302 + 593 = 2,803.
   The increase expressed as a percentage is (2,803 – 2,469)/2,469 * 100 = 13.52% and to the nearest 4% is 14%.

4. The average sales for Ericsson in thousands between 1996 and 2000 is (294 + 493 + 548 + 598 + 632)/5 = 513,000.

5. Scan the table for all five mobile companies and you will find that Cellnet sales were 366,000 in 2000 compared to 120,000 in 1996, which is approximately three times and is the correct answer.

6. Scan the table for the three multiple choices: Orange, Ericsson and Nokia, and don't waste time by calculating others not included.
   The lowest increase in sales in thousands for Orange between 1997 and 2000 was 366 – 232 = 134, for Ericsson 632 – 493 = 139 and for Nokia 1,187 – 679 = 508. Therefore Orange has the lowest increase in sales volume in 2000 as compared with 1997.

Table 4.4 EU members' statistical information in 2000

1. Again, only perform the calculation for the three countries given in your multiple choices and don't waste time.

   Number of people in millions below the poverty line in France: 16% * 60 = 9.6.

Number of people in millions below the poverty line in the UK: 16% * 58 = 9.28.
Number of people in millions below the poverty line in Spain: 19% * 38 = 7.22.

Therefore France has the highest number and A is correct.

2. Let *x* be the total unemployment (men and women), then for Italy: Total employment/Total unemployment in millions = 12/3 = 20/*x*.
   x = 5 million unemployed (men and women), from which 52.2% * 5 = 2.61 million are unemployed women and 5 – 2.61 = 2.39 million are unemployed men.

3. Let *x* be the total unemployment (men and women), then for Belgium: Total employment/Total unemployment in millions = 8/3 = 5/*x*.
   x = 1.875 million unemployed (men and women), from which 1.875 * 30.5% = 0.57 million are unemployed women.

4. We cannot say, because there is no information in the table that gives any details of unemployed men or women aged 60 or over. The table has only general unemployment figures; therefore, we cannot answer the question.

5. The ratio of population between France and Portugal in millions: 60/10 = 6/1 = 6:1.

6. Total employment/Total unemployment in millions in Spain: 3/2 = 19/*x*; *x* = 12.66.
   60.8% * 12.66 = 7.697 million women and **4.9627** million men unemployed.
   Total employment/Total unemployment in millions in Greece: 5/2 = 6/*x*; *x* = 2.4.
   57.5% * 2.4 = 1.38 million women and **1.02** million men unemployed.

Total employment/Total unemployment in millions in Germany:
9/3 = 34/*x*; x = 11.33.
58.5% * 11.33 = 6.629 million women and **4.703** million men unemployed.
Total employment/Total unemployment in millions in Portugal:
2/1 = 5/*x*; *x* = 2.5.
49.5% * 2.5 = 1.237 million women and **1.2625** million men unemployed.

It is clear that Spain has the highest and Greece the lowest number of unemployed men.

Afterword

I hope you have enjoyed reading my book and that it has helped you to build confidence before attending your test. However, remember that if you don't do well on a test it is not the end of the world. This has nothing to do with your intelligence. Look around and you will see that many successful people in public today probably never sat psychometric tests and might well also fail if they tried to take one. It may be that you were tired or moody, or that the weather affected your concentration, or possibly other environmental influences or even your genetic makeup had an effect; if so, other jobs may be more suited to your talents. Good luck.

Further Reading from Kogan Page

Career, Aptitude and Selection Tests, Jim Barrett, 1998
Great Answers to Tough Interview Questions, 5th edn, Martin John Yate, 2001
How to Master Personality Questionnaires, 2nd edn, Mark Parkinson, 2000
How to Master Psychometric Tests, 2nd edn, Mark Parkinson, 2000
How to Pass at an Assessment Centre, Harry Tolley and Bob Wood, 2001
How to Pass Computer Selection Tests, Sanhay Modha, 1994
How to Pass Graduate Psychometric Tests, 2nd edn, Mike Bryon, 2001
How to Pass Numeracy Tests, 2nd edn, Harry Tolley and Ken Thomas, 2000
How to Pass Selection Tests, 2nd edn, Sanjay Modha and Mike Bryon, 1998
How to Pass Technical Selection Tests, 2nd edn, Mike Bryon and Sanjay Modha, 1998
How to Pass the Civil Service Qualifying Tests, Mike Bryon, 1995
How to Pass the Police Initial Recruitment Test, Harry Tolley, Ken Thomas and Catherine Tolley, 1997

How to Pass Verbal Reasoning Tests, 2nd edn, Harry Tolley and Ken Thomas, 2000

Readymade CVs, 2nd edn, Lynn Williams, 2000

Readymade Job Search Letters, 2nd edn, Lynn Williams, 2000

Test Your IQ, Ken Russell and Philip Carter, 2000

Test Yourself!, Jim Barrett, 2000

The Times Book of IQ Tests: Book one, Ken Russell and Philip Carter, 2001

The Times Graduate Job-Hunting Guide, Mark Parkinson, 2001